THE FARMINGTON COMMUNITY LIBRARY
FARMINGTON BRANCH
23500 LIBERTY STREET
FARMINGTON, MI 48335-3570
(248) 553-0300

The Best
Men's Stage Monologues
of 2008

D1316289

MAY 2 6 2009

Smith and Kraus *Books for Actors*
MONOLOGUE AUDITION SERIES
60 Seconds to Shine V1: 221 One-Minute Monologues for Men
60 Seconds to Shine V2: 221 One-Minute Monologues for Women
60 Seconds to Shine V3: 101 Original One-Minute Monologues
60 Seconds to Shine V4: 221 One-Minute Monologues from Literature
60 Seconds to Shine V5: 101 Original One-Minute Monologues for Women
    Ages 18-25
60 Seconds to Shine V6: 221 One-Minute Monologues from Classic Plays
The Best Men's / Women's Stage Monologues of 2007
The Best Men's / Women's Stage Monologues of 2006
The Best Men's / Women's Stage Monologues of 2005
The Best Men's / Women's Stage Monologues of 2004
The Best Men's / Women's Stage Monologues of 2003
The Best Men's / Women's Stage Monologues of 2002
The Best Men's / Women's Stage Monologues of 2001
The Best Men's / Women's Stage Monologues of 2000
The Best Men's / Women's Stage Monologues of 1999
The Best Men's / Women's Stage Monologues of 1998
The Best Men's / Women's Stage Monologues of 1997
The Best Men's / Women's Stage Monologues of 1996
The Best Men's / Women's Stage Monologues of 1995
The Best Men's / Women's Stage Monologues of 1994
The Best Men's / Women's Stage Monologues of 1993
The Best Men's / Women's Stage Monologues of 1992
The Best Men's / Women's Stage Monologues of 1991
The Best Men's / Women's Stage Monologues of 1990
One Hundred Men's / Women's Stage Monologues from the 1980s
2 Minutes and Under: Character Monologues for Actors Volumes I, II, and III
Monologues from Contemporary Literature: Volume I
Monologues from Classic Plays 468 BC to 1960 AD
100 Great Monologues from the Renaissance Theatre
100 Great Monologues from the Neo-Classical Theatre
100 Great Monologues from the 19th Century Romantic and Realistic Theatres
The Ultimate Audition Series Volume I: 222 Monologues, 2 Minutes & Under
The Ultimate Audition Series Volume II: 222 Monologues, 2 Minutes & Under
    from Literature
The Ultimate Audition Series Volume II: 222 Monologues, 2 Minutes & Under
    from the Movies
The Ultimate Audition Series Volume II: 222 Comedy Monologues,
    2 Minutes & Under

To receive prepublication information about upcoming Smith and Kraus books and information about special promotions, send us your e-mail address at info@smithandkraus.com
with a subject line of MAILING LIST. *Call toll-free (888) 282-2881 to order or visit us at
SmithandKraus.com.*

30036010340063

The Best
Men's Stage Monologues
of 2008

Edited and with a Foreword by
Lawrence Harbison

MONOLOGUE AUDITION SERIES

A SMITH AND KRAUS BOOK

Published by Smith and Kraus, Inc.
177 Lyme Road, Hanover, NH 03755
SmithandKraus.com

© 2009 by Smith and Kraus, Inc.
All rights reserved
Manufactured in the United States of America

CAUTION: Professionals and amateurs are hereby warned that the plays represented in this book are subject to a royalty. They are fully protected under the copyright laws of the United States of America, and of all countries covered by the International Copyright Union (including the Dominion of Canada and the rest of the British Commonwealth), and of all countries covered by the Pan-American Copyright Convention and the Universal Copyright Convention, and of all countries with which the United States has reciprocal copyright relations. All rights, including professional, amateur, motion picture, recitation, lecturing, public reading, radio broadcasting, television, video or sound taping, all other forms of mechanical or electronic reproductions such as information storage and retrieval systems and photocopying, and the rights of translation into foreign languages, are strictly reserved. Pages 95-97 constitute an extension of this copyright page.

First Edition: February 2009
10 9 8 7 6 5 4 3 2 1

Cover illustration by Lisa Goldfinger
Cover and text design and production by Julia Hill Gignoux

The Monologue Audition Series
ISBN-13 978-1-57525-620-7 / ISBN-10 1-57525-620-7
Library of Congress Control Number: 2008941387

NOTE: These monologues are intended to be used for audition and class study; permission is not required to use the material for those purposes. However, if there is a paid performance of any of the monologues included in this book, please refer to the Rights and Permissions pages 95–97 to locate the source that can grant permission for public performance.

CONTENTS

FOREWORD

In these pages, you will find a rich and varied selection of monologues from recent plays, almost all of which have been published and are thus readily available to you when you have found that perfect monologue to work on in class or to use for auditions. Many are for younger performers (teens through thirties) but there are also some excellent pieces for men in their forties and fifties, and even a few for older performers. Many are comic (laughs), many are dramatic (generally, no laughs). Some are rather short, some are rather long. All represent the best in contemporary playwriting.

Several of these monologues are by playwrights who have achieved considerable prominence, writers such as Horton Foote, Lee Blessing, David Mamet, Theresa Rebeck, Kia Corthron, and José Rivera; others are by exciting up-and-comers such as Itamar Moses, Qui Nguyen, Ron Fitzgerald, Brett C. Leonard, Kate Fodor and Young Jean Lee.

Most of the pieces included in this book are from published scripts, available from the publishers who also handle performance rights (see the Rights and Permissions section in the rear of this book). In the case of plays which have not yet been published, contact the author's agent for a copy of the entire text.

Break a leg!

— *Lawrence Harbison*
Brooklyn, N.Y. 11232

THE ACTOR
Horton Foote

Seriocomic
Horace, fifteen

Horace is bitten by the acting bug.

HORACE: I hate it when somebody calls me Rudolph Valentino. I was
walking in front of Rugeley's Drugstore yesterday on the way to the
post office when old blowhard Mayor Armstrong came out of the
drugstore and called out in a loud voice, "Hey there, Valentino,"
and all the old men sitting in front of the drugstore laughed like it
was the funniest thing they had ever heard. I didn't think it was
funny at all, but I pretended like I did and I just said, "Pretty well,
thank you, Mr. Mayor" and walked on. When I went to the store
to watch it, so my daddy could go for his afternoon coffee, I told
him about the mayor calling out, "Hello, Rudolph Valentino," as I
went by and he said I shouldn't be sensitive, that he was just being
friendly. Maybe so, but I'm not so sure and I still don't like it.
    . . . Hey. This Rudolph Valentino business all started, you know,
when I won the prize for the best actor at the State Drama Festival.
They gave me a medal for being the best actor, but my teacher, Miss
Prather, accepted it for the school and it's been two weeks since the
Festival and she still hasn't given my medal to me. Miss Prather asked
me to meet her after school. She says she has something for me.
Maybe it's my medal. Anyway, if that's not what she wants I decided today to ask her for it. I hate doing it, but my mothers says she is
a busy teacher and has just forgotten she has it, and she won't mind
at all my reminding her she has it. I hope she won't. Anyway, I'm
going to do it. I want the medal, so I can keep it in my room, and it
will be there to remind me of what it was like when I got the medal.
Miss Prather said it was very exciting when the three judges called
out her name and asked to speak with her and she said she couldn't

imagine what they wanted and when she got to them they said is that Robedaux boy playing the drug addict, afflicted or is that acting? And she said, "It's acting." "Very well," they said, "he gets first prize as best actor," and she said she waited around a few minutes longer hoping they were going to say our one act play won the prize for the best play, but when they handed her my medal and said, "Thank you. You may return to your seat now," she knew we hadn't won best play or best production, only best actor.

ADOPT A SAILOR
Charles Evered

Seriocomic
Sailor, twenties

> *The sailor is talking to a couple with whom he is staying about how*
> *he is less than heroic.*

SAILOR: Hey, you don't have to worry about me dying or nothin'. I'm too awful chicken to die. I hear the sound of a pop gun and I'm just — No, I'm no GI Joe, I could promise you that — So you don't have to worry about — *(Starts to pick up his bag, stops.)* — and it is funny, sir — I mean when you really think about it. I mean, you know, you asking me about why I would go off and — I mean I wish I had some big complicated answer for ya, but to tell ya the truth there just isn't any. I mean I see all those smart people on the Sunday talk shows all talking about the "political" this and that and I hear those movie stars too, you know, talking about why it is they think my buddies and I joined up — and they'll say stuff like they didn't think we had much choice in the matter or that we do it for the money or somethin' like that and I don't mean no disrespect toward them, I don't, but I mean that just makes me laugh. I mean that just makes me chuckle, it does, and I think movie stars are great, but most of the guys I know still can't afford a place of their own — which is why so many of us live on the ship full time anyway. And besides, if we wanted to make the "big" money we'd just go work at Burger King where usually people aren't shootin' at ya. I mean usually, anyway. But I really thought that maybe I could do something, you know, maybe even just help people or something . . .

ADOPT A SAILOR
Charles Evered

Seriocomic
Sailor, twenties

The sailor tells a couple with whom he is staying how he fell out of an airplane without a parachute and survived.

SAILOR: They tell me it was almost five thousand feet, sir.

. . . I just thought it was an interesting fact, ma'am. I thought it would be good to bring up as a part of the dinner conversation.

. . . Oh, it was no big deal, I was just goofin' around with a couple of my buddies in the back of a C-130 awhile back. We were on a training deal with it, learning how to stack up the pallets in back, and the pilot was taking us up for a couple test runs and a couple of my buds and I started horsing around, you know, in the storage area and Tommy Baffuto, a good buddy of mine started to really get on me. He was just pummeling me, you know, climbing up my back, giving me wedgies, the whole nine yards and all I remember was him sort of pushing me real hard up against what I thought was the wall but instead it turned out to be the little side cargo door and "boom" — first thing I know, all I hear is the sound of sucking air and I remember seeing Tommy's face just looking at me kind of strange because apparently somebody forgot to bolt the door and out I went. Boy, that sure was something.

. . . Well after that all of it was kind of a blur. I just remember Tommy's face looking kind of horrified at me. But after I fell through the clouds and started what you might call the "free fall," all of it was kind of beautiful and peaceful to tell the truth.

. . . Well Esperanzo, the doctor from our unit explained it to me later on. He thinks I ended up not dying because of a combination of things.

. . . Well, he said the fact that there was a crosswind, the fact that some old rubber covered telephone lines slowed me down just

4

before I hit the ground and the fact that I landed on a grassy hill just at the right angle. All those things were in my favor, he said.

. . . Plus he said the fact that I was relaxed going down. That I didn't tense up or try to fall on my feet. He said that's what probably saved me in the end. That and the fact that it rained the night before. I made the cross wind a kind of pillow for myself and just kind of leaned back and enjoyed the view.

. . . — and the countryside was awfully pretty. All the rolling hills around the base. And it was late September, so the leaves were just turning.

. . . I stood right up. I just got right up and started walking across the field like nothing happened at all. As it turns out I did break quite a few bones in my leg and about forty or fifty in my back and shoulders, but the doc told me that adrenaline had kicked in by then — and that made it possible for me to just walk across the field and right into the ambulance. One thing I'll never forget is how those ambulance guys just looked at me. They just stood there, staring at me while I climbed all by myself right into the back of the ambulance. They even turned the siren off. And the farmer who owned the field I fell in, he came out to look at me too. And all the time, nobody said a single word. And for days after that people just sort of stared at me, and some even came up to me and touched me on my arm or hand or whatever just for good luck. It was quite an event, it really was. It's one of those things I don't think I'll ever forget as long as I live. These tomatoes are delicious, ma'am.

ADOPT A SAILOR
Charles Evered

Seriocomic
Richard, forties to fifties

> *Richard's wife has signed them up for a program called "Adopt a Sailor," much to his annoyance. Here he is talking to the sailor who is staying with them.*

RICHARD: Mock if you will, but you can't deny what is obvious here. In walks this stranger into our midst. He has come unawares. The night, the very night before his impending journey into what? Before he goes where? Do you realize millions have gone before you? It's as old as time itself and a self fulfilling prophecy. And why? To do what? To kill whom? To save what? Hear the sound of clanging? What is that? It's the sound of metal on metal, man, that's what. It's the ball bearings and pistons. Because what are we, but ghosts in the machine? And how are we less culpable? "Adopt a Sailor?" What is that? I'll tell you what it is. It's the period on the end of a sentence written into ancient templates eons and eons ago so that we could keep the chain of unbroken complicity well oiled and pliable, that's what. "Cocoa Puffs or chicken," what difference does it make? Trace it back.

   . . . Well come on, it's obvious: fresh faced kid sits in the middle of the room eating Cocoa Puffs. Seems benign enough, unless you do a little detective work.

   . . . — sent here, however innocently it might seem, to have himself one more little taste of the life he's been indoctrinated into believing he has to fight and die for. Have some apple pie, kid. Have some ice cream too. Trace it back. Born to live, work, fight, consume, die, live, work, fight consume, die and for what? What are you gonna die for Turkeyscratch? Huh? What are you gonna die for?

BOATS ON A RIVER
Julie Marie Myatt

Seriocomic
Jonathan, twenties

Jonathan desires to do some good in the world despite what his parents say.

JONATHAN: I've got a direct line . . . I'll let everyone know what's going on. I'm doing it by the books. Whatever the hell that means here. But I can't get one goddamn person to return my call. I think the police are laughing behind my back . . . I do . . . Turds . . . And I've already got people asking for money and favors . . . What a fucking headache . . .

. . . You'd probably be interested to know, that my boss told me, as he was tearing me a new asshole . . . "but giving me a chance to prove him wrong" . . . that he's not sure I'm cut out for this kind of work.

(Jonathan takes in the courtyard.)

Hell. My father told me point blank I wasn't as he was dropping me off at the airport.

(Using a thick Texas accent.)

"Son, why do you have to go across the goddamn ocean to prove that you want to help the needy and change the world? America has poor people and prostitutes, don't we? . . . Have you been to Las Vegas? . . . You can help them, can't you? . . . You just don't have the personality of those folks working for Oxfam and Unicef and so forth, son. They're scrappy. They're tough. Doctors, not lawyers. They're skinny vegetarians who don't mind a bug bite or two while they're picking snot out of some starving baby's nose or shoveling shit from a john . . . You don't even like your, your shoes to get scuffed, son. You're uptight. Got a B+ on your report card once and cried for a month . . . You're afraid of failure . . . You

7

hate change. You're impatient . . . Your house looks like a goddamn ad from your Mother's *Good Housekeeping* magazine. Dirt and women and kids make you nervous. If I didn't know better, I might think you're a fairy . . . "

CAGELOVE
Christopher Denham

Dramatic
Sam, twenties to thirties

*Sam has been asked by Katie to tell her why he is "the guy" for her.
He refuses.*

SAM: No. I'm outta this. I'm not here to pitch myself to you. Cause you
knew — Cause you knew — when I was there — that first night
with you — that was it — that was me. And cause I'm the only one
around here who doesn't fuck around with himself and make himself this big deal for everybody to see how I can just, you know,
flaunt it and say you don't know the first thing about me. Well, I
tell you something, you do. You know the first thing. Cause I give
it to you cause that's just me. I meet somebody and, hey, I want em
to know me. Am I so off the fucking mark? I almost got fired today.
I was checking my Hotmail and this is all gonna sound made-up
but there was a junk mail message to me and the subject line was,
"Do you like it rough?" So, I'm figuring, sure, I have about an hour
before I have to work, I'll look at some porn. It's — the first video
— it's this girl tied down to a chain-link fence and guy in a Ken
mask like a mask based on Ken and Barbie — and he's just . . . having his way with this girl. But that's not the disturbing thing. The
disturbing thing is — the girl's like enjoying it. She — so I like kick
my computer — I kick it — and it must have been the angle or
something — but I like really fucked up my toe. And so I make this
noise — like a pain noise — and by this point people are filing into
their cubicles and they all look into my cubicle and they see this
vicious porn and they see me hunched over and moaning. Needless
to say, Leonard told me to go home for the day, after explaining in
detail the company's policy about masturbation in the work place.
So I leave and I have this whole day to fill. And I find myself at a
pay phone, looking through the phone book and for some reason,
I stop when I come to "Private Detectives."

THE CONSCIENTIOUS OBJECTOR

Michael Murphy

Dramatic
Abernathy, forties

> *Abernathy is the Rev. Ralph Abernathy, here urging Dr. Martin*
> *Luther King, Jr. not to come out against the war in Vietnam as this*
> *would certainly be detrimental to their efforts to promote civil*
> *rights at home.*

ABERNATHY: Martin, you and I . . . We've been in this together all the way back to Montgomery, back to the bus boycott, back to the beginnin' . . . And you got to let me tell you: You're movin' too far too fast on this war thing. Sayin' we got to settle this war because you're a man of god is one thing, but . . . Standin' up in a church, in god's house, and puttin' the Communists on the same level as us . . . Or callin' for millions'a young men, black and white, to defy their country when she calls . . . Goin' too far, Martin. And I don't say that like I'm Whitney Young or Roy Wilkins. I say that as your brother, Martin, 'cause that's how I think'a myself, your brother, 'cause you've said it yourself, we love each other like brothers. And I say this to you as your brother: Speakin' out against this war was what you had to do, and I understand that, but now I'm tellin' you, it's time to stop.

. . . It's not the same! It's not! 'Cause I remember. I was in Montgomery before you! You just come from Atlanta, just startin' out in your ministry, and I remember the night. You got a knock on your door and you opened that door and there were your people standin' there, people you did not really know yet, but they came to you because they knew the time had come and so had the man who would lead 'em and they said, Reverend King, we need your help, things'a got to change and we'll follow you and we're willin' to do anythin' or go anywhere. The only one knockin' at your door when it comes to this war is him.

. . . You've started a backlash. And I don't see how you can continue to take this upon yourself when your people ain't knockin' at your door askin' you to lead 'em against this war.

THE CONSCIENTIOUS OBJECTOR
Michael Murphy

Dramatic
LBJ, sixties

> *President Lyndon Johnson is apoplectic that Dr. Martin Luther*
> *King, Jr. is going against him regarding the war in Vietnam.*

LBJ: That goddamn nigga preacher! Gonna get me thrown out'a office!
And after all I done for his people!
(A moment passes.)
    The Harvard boys were in here earlier. They think I'm overre-
actin'. "Mr. President, you don't have to worry about what King
says or doesn't say about Vietnam." See, the Harvard boys have
studied this thing! Pulled out all their charts. Secretary McNamara
has infected everyone around here! Don't say to your president in a
few words what you can dazzle him with in a few hundred charts!
Those Harvard boys flashin' so many charts at me, looked like they
were tryin' to land an airplane 'cross my desk. Nothin' to worry
about, Mr. President, here it is, in black and white: King's people
aren't with him on Vietnam. The Negro supports what we're doin'
over there like every other American, that is, those that don't teach
Marxist Studies at Berkeley. I know you know all this. If J. Edgar
Hoover doesn't have his finger on the pulse of this nation, I don't
know who does. When those boys were finally done with their
charts, there should'a been a drum roll: If King's own people aren't
with him on this, the country's never gonna be! I'm thinkin', somebody, anybody, get some whiskey for my coffee! Pullin' people
together, people who wouldn't normally mix — that's King's spe-
cialty — changin' the way they look at things, gettin' them to think
there's suddenly a virtue in breakin' the law! I don't need no dumb
ass charts to understand that! So, I tell the Harvard boys, I don't

give a flyin' horse fuck about your polls! Don't you understand, you goddamn horn-rimmed morons? King must be stopped! The Harvard boys are just shocked! People think just because I could work with King on some issues of mutual interest that I must trust him. I never trusted him! I got a bullshit detector that goes off when I'm bein' played. It's been known to go off a time or two when the good reverend comes to call. Never mattered, I'm always a step ahead anyway. But I wasn't no step ahead when I got up this mornin', Edgar, was I?

Didn't know about this goddamn speech when I went to bed, no sir! Instead, I get a barnyard full of Harvard bullshit and enough paper to wipe it up! Mr. President, Mr. President, King's hardly made a peep the past year. And he was out of the country. Nobody's payin' attention to him! — meanin' the Harvard boys once again been lulled into their usual stupor sippin' martunies down at the club. To them, one minute, King's in . . . Sittin' on a beach lolly-gaggin'. Working on that goddamn speech! The next minute — he's in New York!

DARWIN IN MALIBU
Crispin Whittell

Dramatic
Huxley, fifties

> *Huxley, a staunch supporter of Charles Darwin, refuses to believe in the Christian God.*

HUXLEY: So where is he? Your Christian God? With all this going on in His name? Because if you ask me, this is a deity who is conspicuous by His absence. Doesn't it ever look to you as if God was the answer to anything we didn't know, and the more we know the less likely He seems to be the answer to anything? I mean He was all over the shop in the early days. In the easy days. You flick through the Old Testament, He's everywhere. Parting seas, bringing down city walls with trumpets. But where is He now? When the assault on Him is so sustained and so compelling? How can you retain belief in a God who's behaving in such a thoroughly unprofessional manner?

. . . If you're asking me to take Him on faith then I think you're asking too much. When Darwin came up with natural selection he didn't just say, "This is how I think it works," and leave it at that. Nobody would have taken him remotely seriously. Least of all you. And you did take him seriously. You would never have been on that podium in Oxford if you didn't. No, you took him seriously because he had evidence. He had his finches, his pigeons, his tortoises and his barnacles. You took Darwin seriously because of his evidence, yet you want me to take God seriously without any. Is it unreasonable of me to ask for evidence, or is it unreasonable of you to demand faith without it? Which is really the sin here? Doubt? Or faith? It . . . it just makes my balls go hard, Bishop! It makes me want to clench my fists, close my eyes, grit my teeth, and jump up and down on the spot going, "Grrrrrrrrrrrrrrrrrrrrr! No! No no no no no no no!" No! No! No,

Bishop! I'm sorry! But no! *(Pause.)* I feel like someone's put a banana in front of me and is telling me it's a giraffe. And I say, "No, it's a banana." And they say, "No, it's a giraffe." And I say, "Look! It's yellow, it's a bit bendy, and it tastes good." And they say, "Yes, it's a giraffe." And I say, "How can you possibly think that?" And they say, "Because it's a giraffe." And I say, "So where's the long fucking neck?" And they reply, "It's a giraffe. That's what I believe. I believe it's a giraffe . . ." And that's where I give up. I just give up.

DIGGING ELEVEN
Kia Corthron

Dramatic
Carter, early thirties, Black

> *Carter's family is having a rare reunion. Here he reminisces about the last time they were together.*

CARTER: *(To Ness.)* The last time we was all together we sat in the baseball bleachers. Hot Labor Day, final picnic the plant threw before cancellin' 'em. You, kindergarten, on the ground takin' Candy by the hand, dancin'. Your gram wearin' the floppy hat. These the days 'fore she went into her head, when we all engaged in the same discussion, and usually she firs' one with the gossip, but today quiet. Not quite a year since your mama died, this a different kinda holiday. Uncle Lee in line for a col' Coke, Ray and I sit back, enjoy the game. Io the star pitcher. Here you come, little mama, bringin' Candy to the bleacher seat. Io's team up now, he and buddies on the bench waitin' to bat. Io take off his shoe, scratch his foot, put shoe back on, he use a shoe horn. Then he smack his next-door buddy's leg with the shoe horn. Buddy tell him quit. He smack it again. "Stop it!" Turn around, he hit his other neighbor on the elbow. Other neighbor give him a look. Io feelin' risky, pushin' the limits. You was a witness, I remember your gigglin', "Look at Io!" You remember?

　. . . This game go on awhile, 'til the shoe horn come up missin'. "Where my shoe horn? Where is my goddamn shoe horn?" Turnin' over the benches and rough friskin' the players, hysterical. They don't get he can't take a joke and he started it, they never seen him like this. I never seen him like this, me and Io not much to say to each other since he's a grown boy, but I long silently admired his cool on the mound, his cool walkin'. Talkin'. Aloof: He got the knack. Now his gram look worried. I go down, talk to him. Get nothin', jus' "Who the hell took my goddamn shoe horn?" I move him to the side. "You wamme getcha another?" "No! I want *that* shoe horn! I want *that* shoe horn!" I go back, investigate. Find the guilty one, I come up with the goods. Give it to Io. I go to leave, to my back Io says, "My mama gimme this shoe horn." Like I ain't figured that out by now.

DOWN AND DIRTY

Lee Blessing

Seriocomic
Vandell, twenties to thirties, Black

*Vandell, a museum guard, talking about some of the strange things
that have happened on the job.*

VANDELL: Someone tried to cut that John Hancock painting. . . . More
crazy mothers come into museums than you think. Thursdays
mostly, when it's free. I like being in that gallery — the Early
American one. Stare at painting after painting. Most of the guards
don't look at the paintings anymore, but I do. You can stare at every
picture in that museum and not even know a brother existed. Early
American — mostly portraits. Everybody looks like they got a stick
up their ass — staring right back at you, never cracking a smile.
Like the smile ain't been invented yet. And, of course, they ain't
even white enough — gotta wear a bunch of white wigs. Standing
there like cut-out dolls. Looks like their whole lives was about finding the one pose they could get into, that they'd never have to get
out of again. That's when I finally understood white people, I think.
Right there in that room. It ain't even their fault. They're born with
it. Got that natural rigidness. Anyhow, old John Hancock used to
hang right down at the end of the room, right next to the door.
Folks never knew who it was 'til they read the little sign. Then I'm
hearing, "John Hancock? Dude that wrote his name big?" "That's
right," I say, "That's him!" Hours on end. Then one Thursday I see
this black guy come in: middle aged. Average looking. He stares at
John Hancock for five solid minutes . . . that's a lot, when you time
it. Then he sits and keeps staring at it, for like half an hour. They
teach us to watch folks like that — ones that look too long. Then
he gets up and stands in front of it again, only a little too close this

18

time. So I slip up closer myself. Just watching. Then he pulls out a box-cutter.

. . . So then I just go all automatic on his ass — you know, jump him, wrestle him down and shit. And he's strong, and I'm trying to get control of that damn blade he's got, and suddenly I'm thinking: "What the fuck am I doing, risking my life to save some racist portrait of some cracker sumbitch from two hundred years ago? Let him cut the damn thing — better than cutting me." I'm about to push him off and get the hell away, when suddenly he goes all weak and drops the box-cutter. I grab it, hold him down. His eyes are kinda funny and I say, "What's wrong with you? Why in hell you want to do a thing like that?" And he says, " 'Cause he's one of 'em." "One of who?" "The Founding Fathers," he says. "What difference does that make?" I ask him — and he says, "I'm one of the bastards. So are you. We all are. We all his bastards."

EAGLE HILLS, EAGLE RIDGE, EAGLE LANDING

Brett Neveu

Comic

Mike, twenties

Mike talks to his friends about why snorkeling is not for him.

MIKE: I don't think I'd like snorkeling.

. . . I can't imagine going underwater and not being able to breathe normally. I can't imagine breathing through that pipe. What if someone were to put something in the pipe? Someone could come by and put something in while you were snorkeling and you'd just go on snorkeling, then you suddenly wouldn't be able to breathe. Maybe someone would put some sort of liquid in your pipe, then you would swallow it and get sick or something. What if you didn't just want to swim on the surface, what if you wanted to swim deeper to get a good look at a fish or a rock or something? I suppose you could scuba dive, but I've heard of people getting the bends, right, the bends? You get the bends and your eyes pop and they get all red with blood, and you get stomach cramps. I hear that then your muscles tighten and you can't swim, and if you're at the bottom of the ocean and you're scuba diving and you get the bends, you're in trouble because you can't move, and you can't see and you're throwing up into your breathing tube. It's like your body explodes. I heard that it's the pressure of all that water, all of those gallons of water pushing down on you as you swim, and if you're not prepared, then it squashes you like a giant cement block. I can't imagine going into the water and thinking to yourself that might happen to you, how could you get in? You'd have to be thinking whatever the opposite of being squashed is, possibly the feeling of freedom that swimming in a large body of water might give you, but it seems overwhelming to me to even gauge one over the other. I know I'd be thinking, "Giant cement block!" I'd stay on the boat, or better yet, I'd be on the shore. In a chair on shore, or maybe in town.

ECHOES OF ANOTHER MAN

Mia McCullough

Dramatic
Dr. Park, forties to fifties

Dr. Park talks about a freak accident he had while performing surgery.

DOCTOR PARK: *(Ruefully.)* Aren't I? *(Long pause.)* When I was doing my residency, I hurt my hand. I . . . I used to carry a scalpel in my coat pocket. The plastic cap that covered the blade came off and the blade poked through the fabric of my coat. I was just bringing my hand down to my side. After gesturing, something simple. I saw this red fluid hitting the floor in front of me in this pulsing spray, and it took me a minute to realize it was *my blood.*

I had some nerve damage. They did a couple of surgeries, but they weren't sure if I'd regain full range of motion. For a time, a couple of months, I didn't know if I could be a surgeon anymore. Some days I wasn't sure if I wanted to be a surgeon. I finally had an out. A reasonable excuse.

You know, your career, your life is on this path and you gather momentum to the point where you can't get off the path without hurting yourself. It doesn't matter if you're wildly successful or mediocre, you're still a slave to that momentum. But if fate steps in and suddenly stops everything — you slice a nerve, you get a brain transplant — then while you're stuck there in that place of recovery . . . you can either feel trapped there, or you can take a really good look at your life and the path you're on. Because it's not dangerous to turn off and take another road now that you're stopped. Recovery can be an opportunity to rediscover yourself. . . . *If* you don't spend all your time being so angry that you can't move.

THE EMPEROR OF ICE CREAM; OR THIRTEEN WAYS OF LOOKING AT DONALD RUMSFELD

Matt Moses

Comic
Rumsfeld, sixties

> *Donald Rumsfeld is giving a "rah-rah" speech to the troops, which gets increasingly surreal.*

RUMSFELD: You need to know that when the history books are written, you will be in them! You are a part of history! The layabouts and the Johnny-Video-Games, they can stay at home. They can sit out history. But you know what? Their deeds won't be in the books. They won't be remembered. You. Will be remembered.

You know, earlier today I met Corporal Graham Dunn's little girl Faith. And do you know what she said to me? She was a little sweetie — she said, "I hope you make all those people happy over there." And you know what I said? "We are going to make all those people happy!"

We talk about freedom, you always hear "freedom freedom freedom" — but, and I know it's family day, but it's just us soldiers in here now — so let me say: *fuck freedom.*

What we're giving these people is happiness. There it is, plain and simple. Think of their lives before. But really think about it. You've got Uday and Qusay running around.

Rape. I mean that's what we're talking about. Innocent women running around. *Innocent women.* Think about your families on the lawn outside this building. Eating coleslaw. Having a hot dog. Your wives.

And the mothers among you — as well as the fathers — think

about your little girls. Your daughters out there having pistachio ice cream cones. *(Gravity. Then light tone.)* I don't know if we actually have pistachio!

Gonna have to — do your daughters like pistachio? I don't know. Ha ha. Maybe I just said it cause I wish they had pistachio.

You know, the only emperor is the emperor of ice cream!

Do you know that one? One of my favorite poems. An American named Wallace Stevens wrote it.

Call the roller of big cigars,

The muscular one, and bid him whip

In kitchen cups concupiscent curds.

We are that roller with the big cigar. The muscular one. And we will make them ice cream.

You all know how hot it can be there — and you know how shaky the power grid is, how they live without electricity. A country like that. With that much oil. And people are living without power. Does that make sense?

And no power, what does that mean? No ice cream. And what is ice cream? Happiness.

Let be be finale of seem.

The only emperor is the emperor of ice-cream.

Let being — let our creating reality — be the ending of "seeming," the finale of mere imagination.

Some would accuse us — America — of being an emperor. And to them I say yes. We are the emperor of ice cream. We are the emperor of happiness.

FALL FORWARD

Dan Reitz

Dramatic
Man 1, twenties to thirties

Speaker is talking to his sister about an event which occurred during their childhood.

MAN 1: They're not necessarily bad dreams. They're just dreams. It's just . . . I wake up, I come down here . . . it brings things up. I thought were taken care of. Is all. *(Pause.)* Also. Saturday's her birthday. Would have been.

. . . Is. *(Pause.)* In the dream I had last night we were kids again, but we weren't little. We were grown up. We were on a lake. I was wearing this skimpy little kid's blue swimsuit with a belt and a big orange life preserver around my neck. She was in this white dress. She was teaching me how to dive. She said, "Look, it's easy, you just lean forward and let yourself go. Like this." She leaned forward with her arms out in front of her, and went in. I waited for her to come back up. I waited. She didn't. I didn't feel panic. I just waited. And then I thought, well, I better go in, too. I went in, I imitated her. I hit the water. But I couldn't sink. Because of this big orange life preserver. I was just . . . bobbing. *(Pause. Takes from his jacket pocket a small Ziploc bag.)*

. . . *(Opens the bag, takes out a small paper napkin.)* Cocktail napkin. *(Reads.)* Notes Taken Observing My Brother On His Birthday: You're never not all business, caught up in making some deal. Always on the make. Right now I'm watching you charming a double-sister act. Or so they say they're sisters. And watching you, if it were anyone else, I'd say oh brother. But you *are* my brother. I recall how, once, when we were kids, you got into a state when Mom and Dad left us with a babysitter and you threw up all over her. So knowing you around your bravura makes your bravura so much more tender to me. I watch you now in this bar on the Bowery, on your twenty-first birthday, in all your male machinations, and I am absurdly proud. Dylan's playing on the jukebox. You're trying to sing along to what you think you hear, Dylan-style, and you make a bad blunder. You sing, "I'm gonna lick your ass . . ." One of them bursts out laughing, "He's not singing, 'I'm gonna lick your ass.' He's singing, 'I'm gonna let you pass.' " They both burst out laughing. You blush to die for. They're in love with you at this moment as much as I am, but for different reasons. Your admiring, loving sis forever. 8/29/01.

FOOD FOR FISH
Adam Szymkowicz

Comic
Bobbie, twenties

Bobbie, an aspiring writer, rants about his latest rejection letter.

BOBBIE: *(In his apartment, takes a letter out of an envelope. He reads it.)*
What? You fucker! You worthless fucker! *(Bobbie paces, he looks at the letter again. He crumples it up and throws it. He pounds the desk in anger, then puts a new sheet of paper in the typewriter. He types.)* Dear Sir, did you even read my masterpiece? If you had, you would not be sending me this form letter of rejection. Not unless you are indeed a complete and worthless moron. I do not accept you as an arbiter of real talent. I have more talent than all of you put together if it comes to that! You with your hackneyed conventions, have usurped the foremost places in art and consider nothing genuine and legitimate except what you yourselves do. Everything else you stifle and suppress. I do not accept you. I do not. It was optimistic of me to think that you were not an undiscerning fool.

Are you all conspiring against me, you with your form letters on separate letterheads that converge into one voice? As punishment for this, your highest crime, know that you have pushed me to eschew publication altogether. Know that you and the others and the world at large will miss out on the rest of my work which I shall never again let you touch with your dirty and destructive hands. My work belongs to eternity now. To the universe of ephemera. But never to you. May you find your just punishment knowing you have kept another genius from the hungry world who aches to hear him. Sincerely, The Author Who Would Have Made You Famous.

THE FOUR OF US
Itamar Moses

Seriocomic
David, twenties

David tells his best friend about a girl he recently met in a bar.

DAVID: I mean, it was very, very easy to talk to this girl. Well, and this one thing especially was really kind of cool, which was that . . . and, I mean, never ever previously in my life have I not had to make the first move. I mean, to not have to actually do the leaning in and the kissing myself . . . I mean, I don't mean *always,* obviously, like not *within* an ongoing *relationship,* of course not, girls will initiate . . . things, but I mean the *very* first kiss with someone new, but with this girl . . . I was in, like, mid-sentence, and she leans in and kisses me. That has never happened to me before. And we just start making out. And then we left the bar, and, you know how all summer it's been so maddening to watch like eight dozen couples making out on the Charles Bridge every night, and wondering: "Where the hell are these people *finding* each other?" It's been maddening for me, maddening, so I made *sure* on the way home to cross the Charles Bridge and make out with her on it, like, *fuck you,* you fucking *backpackers,* and, don't get me wrong, it was really sweet, and, of *course* we're totally exoticizing each other, like the very *fact* of her accent is enough to make her attractive to me, though, I mean, *you* saw her, she was super cute. And even though I kind of got the impression that she doesn't feel so good necessarily about where she is in her, I guess, *real* life, maybe career-wise, like she works in a museum and didn't sound very excited about it, but while she's here in Prague with her friends she could feel how, in my eyes, she's just this sort of dark-haired, dashing British girl. And it worked the other way, too. Because . . . and she *said* this to me at one point, she *said* this, and I thought it was just so sweet, she said:

27

(British accent.) "You're the nicest American I've ever met." And I thought: who has she met? Those . . . backpackers on the bridge. Those blond guys from football schools in Florida. And I felt . . . I was like, "Yeah. Yeah." I felt like: "I represent the very best qualities of my nation." The ones not in evidence in most of the, I guess, *ambassadors* we send out internationally, but here I am, sort of an anomaly, to say: "No. We are also like this." I felt . . . really proud. Oh, oh, and *this* was the coolest thing. Well, because she works in a museum, she knows a lot about art, you know, about architecture, and I talked to her about my play that I'm working on? About Ruskin, uh, John Ruskin, and, but, so, you know, the architecture in this city is so gorgeous, and so we're talking about the buildings, and I talk to her all about . . . like, OK, how, like: the ability to make a, you know, a crenallated . . . whatever. Spandrel. As an ornament for a *building*. And how, like, a really good, adult *craftsman* could make, you know, eighty *thousand* of those in a row that are all beautiful in exactly the same way, but some other part of you, the, like, child who knows nothing, is like: "Hey! Forget spandrels!" And, you know, shock and horror: "But we've been making crenellated spandrels for five-hundred years.!" But, no, like: "Screw *that*. What about, um . . . some acanthus leaves?" But, you know, then it's the craftsman in you that has to execute. Because maybe it *is* a good idea, but if you can't pull it off, you know, people will say, "See? Spandrels are the only way to go, just like we've always known." People will say, "Will you look at that stupid kid? Oh, well, he'll grow out of *that*." And it's like, "No. No. Please don't. Just give him time to learn how to *execute*." And how, Ruskin says, you sort of have to somehow combine those two mutually exclusive things, the craftsman and the child, to really . . . build good buildings. To have . . . both at once. That's . . . genius.

THE FOUR OF US
Itamar Moses

Seriocomic
David, twenties

David may have met The Girl, or so he thinks.

DAVID: I've been seeing this girl. I don't know. Here's the thing. Here's
what's so weird, is, it happened this one night, in this one *moment*,
really, it . . . uh . . . Okay. We're lying in bed together, you know
. . . after . . . and we're going to sleep, and I just have this thought,
this one, stray, like, rogue, thought, just creeps in, just sort of flits
across my brain, and the thought is: what if I feel absolutely nothing for this person. That was it. That was the thought. What if I felt
nothing. And suddenly. I mean. It was like my heart . . . stopped.
Or like I fell through ice. Or like. If my life was a movie? Like I was
the hero, and I had *won*, I got the girl, and the credits rolled, and,
but, instead of it being over, and me being allowed to get up and,
you know, *leave,* instead I was still stuck in the movie, and, even
worse, everybody around me still believed the movie was real, and
was still in character, and I had to, like, play along, but with no
actual sentiment behind it, I mean, seriously, I just wanted to turn
to her right there, in the dark, and say, "Hey. Remember when I
said I loved you? What a great scene *that* was. Okay! That's a wrap!
Maybe we'll work together again someday!" Only I can't do that. I
mean: obviously. I mean: I don't want to *want* to. Because until like
a second before that, literally, like a second before, everything felt
so . . . good. Just . . . fine. And then I have this one thought and
everything just, like, inverted, like a photo negative, or . . . And not
just with this girl but suddenly I started seeing everything this way.
From that moment. I, literally, I have been literally dividing my life,
you know, mentally, into the moment before I had that thought,
and the moment after I had that thought. This one . . . *thought.*

THE FOUR OF US

Itamar Moses

Seriocomic
David, twenties

> *David, an aspiring playwright, is having his first production at a*
> *small theatre in Indiana. The one critic in town has panned his*
> *play. He is at a "talk-back" with the audience, answering their*
> *questions when he finally loses it and launches into a rant about*
> *this critic.*

DAVID: Okay, let's be honest here, I mean, it's not exactly like the people
writing those reviews knew what the fuck they're talking about,
OK? I mean, you can write with a, like, faux-British inflection, and
wear a bow-tie all you want, you're still a critic for some tiny paper
in Indiana, OK? I mean, no disrespect, I just mean: Okay: Please
stop using my *biography* as an excuse not to pay attention to what I
actually *wrote.* Yeah, I'm young. So what's wrong with my play? It's
young. Why? Because that is the *safest fucking thing you can possibly*
say. And so you'll do the safe thing because you're lazy. And you're a
coward. Because *then,* as soon as it's *safe:* everybody comes out of
the woodwork to praise you! Right when it doesn't *mean* anything!
Brilliant, a tour-de-force, *now* youth is somehow this great *selling*
point, *now* it makes the work *vibrant* and *clear-eyed,* it's *only possible*
for someone so gloriously *young,* right? *No.* You're *still* lazy. You're
still a coward. Risk something motherfucker! *Risk* something! *(He*
looks to one side.) Oh, I'm making my director uncomfortable. He's
perfectly comfortable with the reviews, however. Because they have
no problems with him. Which is odd. Because he's a charlatan.
You're a *fraud.* You're *faking* it because you can get *away* with it.
With terrible actors on an awful set under crappy lights, I mean,
Jesus, my words have to run this, like, gauntlet of morons, before
anybody gets to *hear* them, and that's somehow *my* fault? Where are

you going? Oh, did I hurt your feelings? Was it *painful* to be *exposed* in front of an *audience?* Well, there's a first time for everything. Fucker. Get off my stage. I hate you. That is so totally appropriate that you should leave me alone up here because that's the way I feel *already. (Beat.)* Any other questions? Yeah. I'm just *bitter,* right? Well big fucking surprise. I mean: *This is supposed to be fun. Not,* uh, uhhh: excruciating! You know what the first sign is that an event is bad for a writer? You have to wear a *suit* to it. Swanky opening night? Bad. Award ceremony? Bad. The fact that I need an *agent,* some guy to be in a suit *for* me, and watch over the scruffy kid in me, and, like, protect me from getting *screwed,* the fact that I even *need* that: don't you see that that's *killing* us? That that's turning us into *cynics?* This is not why I started doing this. This is . . . I just . . . I just want . . . I want . . . *(Then, quietly.)* Why don't you . . . *risk* something?

GARY
Melinda Lopez

Dramatic
Gary, twenties

Gary is talking to Cassie about how he felt when he kissed her for the first time.

TOMMY: I'm standing here, and it's like I've never seen you before. Never been on this street. Like these aren't my hands. Last night you and me went to the boat landings. We drank some beer. I brought you home. I kissed you — an amazing kiss, the world's best fucking kiss — and I went home and went to bed. My bed. My bed. Please. Tell me you see me here, standing here. Tell me it's me, because I don't know what's happening to the world. The air is poisoned. Look in my eyes.

I watched you grow up, Cassie. When you were eleven, you crashed your bike in our driveway and broke your wrist. I was there. At your first high school dance, you wore a yellow shirt and ribbons in your hair. I was there. I was there the night you and Annie drank so much you threw up in our bathroom. I was there the day your first boyfriend broke up with you, and you cried all night long. I know you too Cassie.

Because I'm different. Because last night when I kissed you, I felt something for the first time in so long. Because when I was walking to work this morning, the sky was blue. And I was thinking about getting out — just getting where the sky is blue all the time. Making something new. Like I could, I don't know it's retarded, but maybe, you know, farm or something. I mean, not farm farm, but like — work outside. Where the air is clean. Have a place. And you were there too, Cassie. You were laughing. There was this blue sky, and you were there. And I was happy. Look at me. Do you see me?

GOOD, CLEAN FUN
Lee Blessing

Dramatic
Denby, twenties, Black

Denby is talking to a co-worker about how he got pulled over while driving to work because he is black.

DENBY: Tell you the truth, it wasn't really a traffic problem. Got pulled over. Not 'cause I was speeding. I was doing five miles *under* the limit. No, I was pulled over 'cause I was black. *(No response.)* Had my eight-hundred dollar suit on. Driving my oh-so-corporate Beamer. Tail lights fine, got the right tags on my plates. Didn't seem to matter. State cop. Flashing lights — woo-woo! — pulled me over. I said, "Why, Officer — what can be the problem?" He said, "Get the fuck out of the car." So I did. I moved slowly — didn't want to spook him. Oh, did I mention he was white? *(No response.)* So I'm smiling, and I would be talking if I hadn't been told to shut the fuck up. Meanwhile he's pulled his gun. He tells me to put my hands on the car and spread my legs. And I do this, remembering that I really haven't done enough stretching recently. His partner's on the other side of the car pointing his gun at my face. The partner's just a kid — trembling, nervous, sweaty trigger-finger. Might've been his first time out. He was white too. Probably just a coincidence. *(No response.)* Anyhow they pull out my wallet, and then the older cop says, "Mr. Denby, eh? That's not a very black name, is it." And I feel the barrel of the gun on the back of my neck, and I say, "It's just a name." *(No response.)* And then there's this really long moment. And I glance up at the young patrolman, who yells, *"Don't look at me!!!"* So I don't. I look at the rear window. I look through it at one of my son's storybooks in the back seat. And I look at my reflection in the rear window: dark, sweating, breathing shallow . . . I'm thinking that time really can stop. Stop on a dime. Just like my car. Just like me. *(No response.)* And then it's over. Wallet flips shut. Gun barrel disappears. "Get outta here. And *watch* yourself." And I want to say something. *But* I think better of it, and get into my car like they tell me and get outta there. They follow me for five more miles. Finally they turn off. *(His tone suddenly becomes breezy.)* And here I am, just a little bit late. Thought I was going to be a lot later than this. The late Mr. Denby, eh? It's almost funny.

GOOD, CLEAN FUN
Lee Blessing

Dramatic
Hewitt, thirties

Hewitt tells about a run-in he had recently with a black woman in a barber shop.

HEWITT: Went somewhere new for a haircut last week. Not my usual joint, some cheap chain place. Should've known better. But in I went. Nobody at the desk. No one getting a haircut, either. Only person in there was sitting in a chair way over by the wall. Noticed her out of the corner of my eye, but I could've missed her completely. Didn't know if she was an employee or a customer. Meanwhile, I'm standing at the desk. Time goes by, she doesn't say a word.

. . . What do you think? Anyhow, finally she asks if I'm there for a haircut, and I say — politely — "Yeah." But I realize I've already done it wrong. This woman doesn't like me, because I didn't notice her at first. I didn't look at her, because — she assumes — she's black. Maybe I thought she was just hanging out, or she's just there to clean up, right? So already she hates me. Does she speak to me even once the whole time she cuts my hair? No. In fact a white girl comes out from in back, and my girl makes a point of talking to her the whole time she's cutting my hair. This black woman's hands are working as hard as they can not to actually touch my head. No scissors — screw the scissors, that would be way too intimate. Clippers. Clippers roaming all over my head like a fucking robot lawnmower while Tonisha or Donisha or Oppalocka, or whatever the hell her name is, gabs away about what they've decided to name the next one. And never do I feel her hands on me. Never do I get the comfort of a haircut honestly delivered. Never do I hear, "How's that look?" She hated me the minute I walked in the door. Because I was white, and male and middle-aged. And I hated her.

GREAT FALLS
Lee Blessing

Dramatic
Monkey Man, forties

> *"Monkey Man" is what the speaker is called by his teenaged step-*
> *daughter, whom he is taking on a cross-country trip against her*
> *will. Here, he talks about his tempestuous marriage to her mother.*

MONKEY MAN: Divorce is no reason to lock people out of your life.
Divorce is . . . normal, and natural, and more people do it than
don't. So . . . So why compound the damage? Why take sides, or
pretend that one partner or the other is an ogre or . . . a villain of
some sort, when the truth is *always* that it's *both* people's fault?
(Nodding, as though someone is responding.)
  I know, I know. I did bad things. I did very unthinking and
heartless things that came out of what was really — what was it?
What was it really? It was *really* . . . Arrested development, that's
what it was. Emotionally, I was still a child. I was incapable of anything like real introspection, or real growth, or real . . . fidelity. But
you know the worst thing I did? I can say this, now that we're being
honest. Now that we're here, face to face. The worst thing wasn't
going outside the marriage, it was . . . it was telling her. Because you
can never do that. You can never think a thing like that will ever do
any good — not the least, tiniest little grain of good. Because we're
all weak. We're all . . . we're subject to it. She told me, your mother told me, when we were in the middle of that entire, mess of *shit*
and *anger* and . . . shame . . . that she flirted with it. She was
romanced by someone. Well, romanced — he was trying to . . . fuck
her, and he was a friend of ours, a very charming and handsome
. . . What? No, I'm not going to say who it was. The point is, the
much larger point — and this is when I realized it by the way, when
it became *clear* to me — is that fidelity is not what people demand

36

from each other in marriage. What we demand . . . No, no — hear me out. What we *demand* is not to be humiliated. Which ninety-nine percent of the time means not to be told. "Honey, I almost slept with that guy. We were sitting, talking on the couch in his apartment. He was so attentive, he really seemed to care. And we'd had some wine —" No. No! "We made out for awhile. It was just kissing, but then —" *No!* We don't do this. We demand from each other not to do this. Because it's humiliating to sit in a conversation and be told that the person you give yourself to gives himself to . . . someone else — under any circumstance. And the point is, I know that *now*. Because . . . and this is what it really is. Under everything. The essence of it. Unless you're having your spouse tailed twenty-four seven by the world's best detective agency. you can *never know for certain* if they've stayed faithful every minute of every day. But what you can know is if they've told you. That you can know. And the reason your mother and I divorced — I think anyway, this is definitely my interpretation — is that I told her. But I didn't have the affairs because I wanted out of the marriage. And I didn't tell her because I wanted out of the marriage. Honestly, that was never — at least until the very end, maybe — that was *never* the reason. I didn't want these revelations to end things. I wanted them to . . . change her. That she would hear these things, and they would wake something up in her. That she'd realize that I didn't enjoy these . . . *activities*, that I was in pain. Every day. I was in pain every day with her, and these . . . lapses, adventures — I don't know what to call them — were a kind of relief that instantly palled. Lost its appeal, became ugly and pointless, instantly, because I didn't love them.

HUNTING AND GATHERING

Brooke Berman

Seriocomic
Astor, twenties to thirties

> *Astor is a Man with a Van, here talking to a woman who might be
> in need of his services.*

ASTOR: Hey. Hi there. Hey.
I'm returning your call.
Got your message.
I want to help.
Let me help.
I charge money
But I get the job done.

You say you need your band equipment
to travel from one side of the city to another?
Easy. I do that.
Precious artwork?
I do that too.
I move those things.
I carry them.
I get them
to where they need to be.
All your things.
Everything you hold
carries energy,
your charge. Your life unfolds
according to what kind of charge
you carry —
and where

you place
that charge
and how much of it
you're willing to let go of,
Change.
That's right.
Evolve.
That's what this is all about.
E-VO-LUTION
Let me help.
It's my business.
I get you there in one piece.
Man with Van. That's me.
The Man with The Van.
I'm the Man.
With the Van.

THE LAST GOOD MOMENT OF LILY BAKER

Russell Davis

Dramatic
Sam, thirties to forties

Sam is talking to Bob, whose wife has told him she is unhappy, trying to give him some perspective.

SAM: There are two things we don't like to talk about. Three things, Bob. Heart attacks, cancer and a wife who's decided somewhere down the road she can't be happy anymore.

. . . things happen, Bob. Lots of things happen. They can leap out of nowhere. We don't even want to admit them, talk about them, nothing, because they can take you out of the picture. And the picture is business. We're meant to do business. It's fun. Every time I take a plane I look out the porthole and there's business. The fields, the desert, they're divided for business. Nothing is any longer just trees and bugs and animals. And there has to be a reason for that. Which is we need to take our minds off the things we can do absolutely nothing about. Like if a car hits into us, or one of our children. Or if the universe expands. Or detracts. Or if a wife goes sad on us. Business is what protects us. Because business is the only thing we have left to keep our attention going and focused on something we can do something about.

(Pause.)

Lily's taking you out of the picture, Bob. From the very beginning she took you out. There was no reason you had to go to state college. You could have gone away. You could have gone to the world.

(Pause.)

Bob, on the way here yesterday we got lost. Molly and I, in the car. And we argued. Our memories clashed on which way we drove fifteen years ago. And finally I pulled into this farmhouse. Nice white farmhouse where there was no more farming. Just two guys living. Young big fellows. Big plaid shirts. Healthy. No wives. And they came out to ask what we wanted. These two guys. So they gave us directions and we drove ahead. But, Bob, it reminded me a hell of a lot, in the deepest way, of what we used to have. When there were directions, simple directions, anywhere you wanted to go, and there were still all these choices. Simple choices. Sometimes I think the promise I had, the expectation, got interrupted when I married Molly.

(Pause.)

I think you should tell me what's going on with your wife.

MASSACRE (SING TO YOUR CHILDREN)

José Rivera

Dramatic
Joe, thirties to forties

Joe shatters the smug complacency of a community.

JOE: You people were given *paradise* . . . fucking *maple* trees, *chipmunks,* intoxicating flowers — like God was breathing on this town, forcing life with every puff of wind. What a gift! And it was just handed to you, so full, so fat, all you had to do was get on your knees and wonder how you got so lucky. Instead, you take the promises made to the earth and cancel them for your own selfish prosperity. You suck her dry and piss in her garden. *(Beat.)* I bet you people never wonder about this town and all the massacres that made it possible. Bet you never asked yourselves: who's haunting the walls of my house? Whose bones are holding up its foundation? Whose tears are pouring through the faucet to thicken my coffee? Whose betrayal made my freedom possible? Whose food supply is fattening my kids? Whose myths have I stolen to write my story? What dumb spirit comes to me at night in the form of a bird or coyote begging to be recognized as the remnant of a conquered race? *(Beat.)* It's all blood, you guys. It's all a lot of blood, going all the way back, and you're swimming in it. Where is God for you people? In the desire you have for each other? In the weapons? In the lies? Is God in the blood you washed off your hands? You thought you were so good — so I had to test you — I set this whole thing up. C'mon! You didn't really think Erik and Panama were smart enough to do this on their own! I set up a test, which all of you failed. I'm so disappointed. How can you put these holes in me and talk about making love and replacing your children? Is God in your bed? There is no God for you! How did I get off on this? Oh yeah, you people make me sick. And I get sick of having to punish you people.

MAURITIUS
Theresa Rebeck

Dramatic
Sterling, forties to fifties

> *Sterling has come to a stamp shop with a suitcase full of money to buy two stamps, misprints from Mauritius, but has found to his dismay that their ownership is in question. He is a rather threatening character, who doesn't want to leave empty-handed.*

STERLING: Hey. They are not your stamps. They are my stamps. There are a few remaining questions involved in this transition, but no one is in doubt about who those stamps belong to. Isn't that right, Dennis?

. . . He talks well, doesn't he? That's one of the things I like about him. I could use a smoke, I feel like smoking. There's something post-coital about moments like this, but I don't want to get ahead of myself. Where the fuck is Philip? Fuck him, he doesn't get here in time to put in his two cents, he's just fucked. He's a moron, he doesn't want to be a part of this. Those stamps are phenomenal. Exquisite, right? Exquisite.

. . . I'm not happy, I'm something else. Fuck yes I'm happy, those stamps are — where'd you find them? Don't tell me I don't want to hear that idiotic story about your dead mother again. Jesus, those are gorgeous stamps. Those stamps aren't out there. Both of them? Uncancelled? They aren't out there. How much does she want for them? No. Don't tell me. I want to hear it from her. You been giving me a lot of trouble tonight, what's your name, Jackie? Jackie, answer me. Is that your name?

. . . It's all been very irritating and I understand that that was your purpose. You know you have something valuable, and you want to make sure I understand that this deal isn't going to be easy to make. You want me off my game, you want to keep me emotional, and you've been very successful so far in that endeavor. I respect that, Jackie, it's a tactic I've used plenty of times myself and I would not have suspected someone as young as you would have such command over this kind of territory. You surprised me, and I don't mind telling you I am not often surprised. Have a seat.

. . . Whatever makes you happy. I don't want to piss you off here. I don't mind telling you, I don't like you when you're pissed. I, however, will sit.

(He does.)

Okay, now you and I are going to talk about what you think you want, from me, as a fair price for those stamps.

. . . Dennis. As I said, I often enjoy listening to you talk, but this needs to be between me and Jackie. What do you want, Jackie? What do you want for those stamps?

. . . You know what Dennis here said about you, when he brought your situation to me? He said, this girl is a lamb. And don't get me wrong. I like Dennis, but he was mistaken when he characterized you that way.

. . . You know what else he said? He said you were damaged. So am I. Neither one of us is a lamb. Now, you don't want to name a figure. That's a good beginning. You make me name the price and then we go up instead of down. But I'll tell you, I'm not going to name a figure, either. What I will do for you is give you the beginning and the end. There are some times in life when everything is about negotiation. What I want, what you want, what Dennis wants, Philip, who knows what he wants or even where the fuck he is, all of that comes into play and then the ending is in question, because the negotiation isn't about the ending, that's why so many questions arise. Are you following this? Don't answer; I can see you are. You and I both know, this isn't about negotiation. You want money, and I want those stamps. Obviously there's more to it than that or you wouldn't be working my nerves the way you've been. You did some research, you found out how much those stamps may be worth?

. . . Good. I'd be embarrassed for you if you hadn't done that. Now I want to explain a few things about commerce, at this level of investment. Stamps like this, they are an investment to people, not a lot of people can afford to shell out several millions of dollars to own a one penny and a two penny post office, but people who can, people to whom something like that might make sense? These stamps are an investment. In a different, more formalized situation, you go through a broker, you hire a couple of experts to authenticate the investment, you pay rather considerable taxes, state, local, federal, you need lawyers, accountants, trust me, no one is going to let you get through a multi-million dollar investment purchase without overhead that many many people consider onerous. Twenty five percent off the top, and that is not off the top of my end, that's out of your end.

. . . So one or two of your many millions has just been lopped off. At the outset. In addition I hope you don't mind my pointing out — you like rules, I heard you mention to Dennis, before, that rules you see as being protections, you're aware of the need for protections? Jackie, you get more formalized, in the hope of gathering to yourself more money in exchange for your valuable product here, and the rules become your enemy. And what I've seen of you, Jackie — neither one of us is particularly at home in situations where there's a lot of fools to suffer. Where a lot of noise enters the equation. Where the intimacy is lost. Because what we're talking about here, Jackie — what is going on between you and me — is the most intimate exchange. People want to lie about that, confuse that, but they are liars and they are obfuscators. You have time for that? Months, years, to waste on a lot of people wanting to participate, to interfere, to degrade what you and I are doing here? Because I don't have months to waste. I don't even have days. I know what I want out of life. And this is it.

. . . Now. This is my understanding of what it is you want. You want money, yes, that is the primary reason you took the chances you did, to come here tonight. But you want more than that. You want respect, and you want recognition for your courage and your determination. Now. I give you that. Yes?

. . . Yes. And I give you this, too.

(He gets the suitcase from behind the counter, brings it out front, and opens it.)

I want you to count it. And decide. The beginning, and the end. No negotiation. This is what I brought here, to make this happen tonight. It is a shitload of money.

It is more money than you ever in your wildest dreams imagined having, at any one point in your young life. Is it what those stamps are worth? Who's to say? It is cash, it is under the table, there's no overhead, there's no lawyers, there's no fucking accountants here, to drive you and me fucking crazy with their nonsense. That's added value; you can't deny it. You also can't deny that at this moment? Those stamps are only worth what I will pay for them. In the future, if you took a chance, could you get more for them, from someone else? Maybe. But I don't live in the future. I live in the present. In my world, the present is the only moment that exists. And this is the only deal that exists. That amount of money. For those two stamps.

MEN OF STEEL
Qui Nguyen

Comic
Jason, twenties

Jason is talking to a woman about how hard it is to be a superhero.

JASON: You don't know what it was like for me, Helen. Having this much power. It's like God kissing every muscle — every joint — every particle which makes up me. I feel nothing of this world. No pain equals no pleasure — both sensations connected by a thread so fine that sometimes you can't tell where one ends and the other begins. All I have is power — this constant throbbing vibration within — a power that I feel eating away at me — a power changing me — evolving me — turning me into something beyond this mortal coil.

They didn't make a hero when they turned me into Captain Justice, Helen. They just recreated the Atom Bomb into the form of a man.

I like being here — being with you. Out there, I walk among eggshells. I tiptoe between dolls made of rice paper careful not to breath too hard, touch too abrasively, embrace anything — anyone — with passion. For if I'm not careful, I'll blow away humanity itself as if it were a Buddhist sand painting.

But here — here the world is safe from me.

And I get to be with you.

MEN OF STEEL
Qui Nguyen

Seriocomic
Lukas, twenties, Black

> *Lukas is ranting to another black man about how things are differ-*
> *ent for blacks as opposed to whites, and how that isn't going to change*
> *even if they hook up with a superhero named "Captain Justice."*

LUKAS: D, your sister ain't talking to you cause you in jail. You in jail cause you shot up a cop — a cop who happened to be her boyfriend. Do you see a connection? Do you see why she might not think fondly on you about this?

. . . Whatever, dawg. I'm going to sleep.

. . . Accidents are what happens when white folks shoot up some-body. They call it "involuntary manslaughter" or "unintentional homicide" or some shit fancy term meaning they ain't going to jail. Folks like us, however — we should just be happy we ain't hangin' by our necks.

. . . Yeah, I'm a bleak motherfucker. I'm a stormy fuckin' cloud. Getting thrown in the pen does that to a motherfucka.

. . . Look, D, I don't give a shit no more. About Captain Justice, Liberty Lady, all them supers — they can go fuck themselves for all I care. Do you know what I want to see? What I really want to see? I wanna see my ratty ass apartment again. Fuckin' Marcus and King acting like fools on the corner. I wanna see your bitch ass sister again — our boys at the bodega — fuckin' Dominican flags hangin' from windows and what not. I wanna see Bushwick. I wanna see home. But ya know what? That ain't gonna happen.

The truth is there's no use to be worrying about Camille or addresses or who misses who. Look at us — look where we at. Everything we are, will be, is this. Nothin. We just a whole lotta wasted nothin'. And that, D, ain't gonna change by meeting Captain J.

NOVEMBER
David Mamet

Comic
Charles, forties to fifties

> *Charles is the President of the United States, up for reelection, and his first term has been a disaster of incompetence. Here he is on the phone to the head of his party, who has not only denied him funds to do any more advertising but funds for his presidential library as well.*

CHARLES: *(Pause.)* Barry, look: you've screwed me on the
election, I need you to disgorge
the funds you're holding for my library.
(To Archer.)
What do I mean "he's screwed me . . . ?"
(To phone.)
What do I mean, Barry? I'm looking
at the time-buys . . .
(Pause.)
Well, whose decision was that,
Barry? "The committee?" Yeah, no,
yes, that's peachy, Barry. With the
possible exception, YOU ARE THE
COMMITTEE. Barry? You . . .
(Pause.)
Well, who the fuck is the
Committee, if not you?
[*(Archer hands Charles a list.)*]
Three spots in Cleveland, two in
Mineapp . . . FOR THE WEEK? FOR THE
WHOLE FUCKEN WWWW . . . WHY DON'T I
JUST GO OUT AND GET CLOWN SHOES, 'N

PUT A RED RUBBER BALL ON MY FUCKEN
NOSE, BE . . . be . . . because I want to:
Fuck that, Barry, because
I'm gonna tell you, no I'm gonna
tell you why, and you can
jolly well sit there. BECAUSE MY
FUCKEN QUESTION TO YOU IS A SPEECH
THAT YOU, and your fucken shooting
party made to me out hunting
quail in Bavaria, when someone turned
to me and he said, "Chucky, have you
read the Three Musk . . ." Well, it
doesn't sound like you're . . . No,
it doesn't sound like you
remember, Barry, when someone asked
me: "All for one and one for all."
You remember that? And all your
tame Krauts, and lifting the import
tariffs, and "This is our man,"
and all that happy horseshit . . .
I DON'T *WANT* a . . .
I DON'T . . . WHAT THE FUCK AM I
GOING TO DO WITH A TIME-SHARE IN
ASPEN? I want to be President . . .
(To phone.)
    . . . Is this the man I knew? In the snow?
In New Hampshire? BARRY, who ruined
his fucken shoes going from door to door?
Is this the same man?
(Pause.)
Well, in what way is he different?
(Pause.)
What does that mean? What does
that mean? "A good one to lose"?
You know who thinks that way?
Losers.

(Pause.)

Let's move on.

Tell me about the library. Well:

oh, OK. Good. "We have a fund."

How much money do we have in my

Library Fund . . .

(Pause.)

Million.

(Pause.)

Thousand?

(Pause.)

Four thousand dollars . . . ?

(Pause.)

I CAN'T GO HOME WITHOUT A LIBRARY

FOR CATHY . . . You know that . . . I

should of thought of that when I

invaded where? When *I* invaded where?

Barr . . . ? Barry, that

was your idea . . . The fuck it was.

The fuck it was. The fuck it was,

Bar, YES I FUCKEN MIND IF YOU PUT ME ON

HOLD . . . ! I am the President of the United States!

(To Archer.)

Where is he? In Nantucket?

(To phone.)

Where are you, on Nantucket?

HOW ABOUT I GIVE AWAY half of the island

to the Micmacs to build their hotel casino.

Yes, I can. Yes, I . . . Yes, I can.

Barry. Well, what are you going to do to me?

(Pause.)

That record was expunged,

(Pause.)

That record was expunged, and the statute

of limitations . . .

(Pause.)

Well, who's to say what's perjury . . . ?

(Pause; to Archer.)

His friend the special prosecutor.

(Pause; to phone.)

Yeah. Alr . . . yeah. Alr . . . Alright . . . Barry.

(Pause.)

And give my best to Ginny.

(Pause; hangs up.)

NOVEMBER
David Mamet

Comic
Charles, forties to fifties

> *Charles is the President of the United States, up for reelection, and his first term has been a disaster of incompetence. Here he is talking on the phone to a lobbyist, who he hopes will give him money for his library. Also in his office are his Chief of Staff and his speechwriter.*

CHARLES: *(To phone.)* Hello, Tink? How they hanging . . . ?
(To Archer.)
Caught between a dick and an asshole.
(To phone.)
That's a good one. Tink . . .
(To Archer.)
Are we calling about that "thing,"
about the piggyplane . . . ?
. . . Tink, far as I know, we've got a clean
board on the *piggyplane* . . .
(To Archer.)
Some guy in Bulgaria wants to file a complaint
to . . . what? The International Amnesty for
Victims of Oppression? They saw the piggy
plane? They saw the people getting off the
plane? Bags over their heads in manacles . . .
How'd they know the plane was yours?
(To Archer.)
They saw the curly thing on the tail.
. . . Who saw it? A reporter?
(He nods.)
Tink? Get me his name and we'll

have him killed. . . . Tink . . . Yeah,
it's been such fun working with you,
too . . . But Tink? Lookit *here*: my *library* . . .
(Pause; to Archer.)
He was thrilled to be able to make
the contribution he made to our . . .
our campaign, and he only wishes it
could have been more.
(To phone.)
Tink: I think I may be able to
make your wish come true. Look
here: Tink: You sitting down? What if. What if:
historically, at Thanksgiving. Americans. DID
NOT EAT TURKEY.
(Pause.)
Well, they ate pork.
(Pause.)
Well, who the fuck knows if they
did or not. There's guys say World
War *Two* never took place.
(Pause.)
I dunno, some *Frenchmen.* Point of my call: Tink.
I got these turkey guys, want me to bless
their turkeys. But — I'd rather go to my friends:
. . . Tink, I would like to use the
power of my office,
to *inform* the American populace
that, from now on. We will *not*
demean, the memory of our ancestors
white *and* red by eating turkey at
Thanksgiving, but . . . hold on, but,
BUT will honor them by eating pork.
(Pause.)
Fuck the Jews.
(To Archer.)
Do the Jews celebrate Thanksgiving?

. . . *(Listens to the phone.)*
Who? . . . well, fuck them, too. How many
Arabs do we *have* here . . . ?
(Pause.)
Oh.
(Pause.)
Jeez . . .
(Pause.)
Well . . .
(To Archer.)
"How about some *other* holiday?"
(To phone.)
Tink, that's not what we're selling.
Tink. *Today* here's what we're selling:
we're selling, on Thanksgiving,
Pilgrims ate pork. Pilgrims ate pork
on Thanksgiving.
(Pause.)
Well thanks anyway.

And "do I want a seat on his Board?"
. . . No, you know what, Tink. Hey, gimme *two* seats on
the Board. You bet. Thanks for listening.
(Hangs up.)
He thinks he "gave" cause he lent
us the piggyplane . . . Sinking ship, sinking ship?
(To himself.)
They didn't eat pork on Thanksgiving . . .
They didn't eat Turkey . . .
(To Archer.)
What about if they ate tuna?

100 SAINTS YOU SHOULD KNOW

Kate Fodor

Dramatic
Matthew, thirties to forties

> *Matthew, a Catholic priest, has been asked to take a leave of*
> *absence after some homoerotic photographs were found in his room.*
> *In this direct address to the audience he talks about those photo-*
> *graphs and the feelings they instill in him.*

MATTHEW: *(To the audience.)* These are the pictures that Mrs. Tierney,
the church secretary, found in my study. They've given me three
months to think about them. Three months to pray and to con-
template while a visiting priest from New Mexico tends to my con-
gregation, and then I'm to meet with the bishop and explain myself.
(He looks at the pictures.) They're by George Platt Lynes, a photog-
rapher who worked in New York City in the 1930s. He photo-
graphed movie stars for magazines, but he also took pictures — he
also took pictures like these ones. I hadn't ever heard of him until I
found a book called *George Platt Lynes* in the public library. I was
looking in the L's in the art section for Lorenzo Lotto, who painted
the lives of the saints on the walls of the Suardi chapel in Trescore
in 1524, and I found *George Platt Lynes* instead. I don't think any
patron of our local library had ever looked at the book before I did.
The edge of each page peeled away from the next one as I turned it,
the way they sometimes do in books that have never been read, as
though you were breaking into something that's meant to stay
sealed. *(A beat.)* I ripped the pictures out of the book. I took the
book to a long table in the back of the library, away from the DVDs
and the Internet access stations to a place in the library that's meant
for reading and so is always utterly deserted, and I ripped out the
pages I wanted. I don't know what came over me. I'm careful with

books. I don't approve of dog-earing pages to mark your place. Not even that. And when I'm reading a book, I hold it open only three-quarters of the way, so as not to crack the binding. But I ripped out the pages and folded them into my pocket, and at home, I opened them and smoothed them with my hands. I think I took them because I felt somehow, just momentarily, at the quiet table in the library, that God was in the pictures. There is a line of thought that goes that beauty is God's goodness made visible, that it's in objects of beauty that we see the beauty of the Lord reflected. When God called me to service, he called me through beauty. In the church, there was incense and quiet. Dark wood. Masses and requiems. I went to talk to Father Michaels, and his study smelled of books, and bits of colored light from the stained glass windows were thrown across the floor like someone had spilled a handful of rubies, and I thought, "For wisdom is better than rubies, and all the things that may be desired are not to be compared to it," and those words were my calling. So one can be called to God by beauty. But I know, also, now, that one can be called away from God by beauty. The Church teaches that as priests we are sanctified: that is, literally, separate, set apart for sacred use. I'm set apart. I'm set aside. I'm lonely. When I look at the pictures, I inhabit the bodies of the men; I don't look at them as objects of desire; I become them, just as a beginning step before even thinking about desire. I feel for the first time since I was a child what it might mean to have a body. Maybe even what it might mean to have a body in relation to another person's body. I look at the pictures, and those lines from St. John of the Cross come to me out of nowhere. "With his gentle hand he wounded my neck. And caused all my senses to be suspended." I didn't even know that I knew them, and suddenly they're all I can find in my head no matter what else I'm looking for. "Upon my flowery breast, Kept wholly for himself alone, There he stayed sleeping, and I caressed him." I know that it's supposed to be about God, but I just can't seem to hear it that way anymore.

(*Blackout.*)

ON THE LINE
Joe Roland

Dramatic
Dev, twenties to thirties

*Dev, a blue collar guy, is talking to his buddies about how he has
no doubts about his life.*

DEV: *(Offstage.) (He comes back on stage and begins to dress.)* Every morning I get up, I know who I am. I know where I'm going, I know what I'm gonna do when I get there and I know who I'm gonna see. I got this sense of being a real goddamned person. I fit. Everything about me fits. Every day I throw on clothes that look just like the clothes I had on yesterday, I grab a quick coffee and I wait for Jimmy and Mikey to come pick me up. Or I jump in my truck and head over to pick them up depending on the week. And every day we stop at the same diner and order the same thing. I get pancakes, scrambled eggs and a side of bacon, coffee with cream; Jimmy gets sunny side up, rye toast and sausages, coffee black, French fries instead of hash browns; and Mikey gets poached eggs, English muffin with either a side of oatmeal or cream of wheat, he alternates between ham and sausage, never bacon, but sometimes he'll swipe a piece of mine. Coffee with skim milk. Why the fuck anybody would drink coffee with skim milk is beyond me. And every day after breakfast we head to the plant, put in eight hours on the line, unless there's overtime to be had, then sometimes it's twelve or more. Depending on the night, we go out. Same places, same people. And every night I go home, lay my ass in bed, and thank sweet Jesus I get to do this shit all over again tomorrow. Far as I'm concerned, soon as I hear that asshole on the radio at 6:30 in the morning I just won the goddamn jackpot, 'cause I get to be me for a whole 'nother day. It's not like I'm full of myself or anything. It's just I know who I am. And there's a certain level of comfort in that.

I guess I'm lucky 'cause I've had this frame of reference my whole life, this gauge to tell me who the hell I am and how far off I might be getting from being me. I've had the same two best friends since I was seven years old. How many of you can say that? You forget who you are they remind the fuck out of you. Like that.

ON THE LINE

Joe Roland

Dramatic
Dev, twenties to thirties

*Dev, a blue collar guy, is talking to his buddies about the power
and the beauty of women's legs.*

DEV: I love legs. I'm not saying I'm a legman. That would be crass. But
there is a power, a true and real power that a pair of beautiful legs
wields over me. I can't breathe, my heart races, my palms sweat and
I feel like I did right before I asked Alissa Liberati to the prom. On
the verge. Suddenly the universe and its possibilities no longer
escape me. In fact it's just the opposite. In the presence of physical
beauty suddenly everything makes sense. I am here to bear witness.
Yes it's true I have fallen in love with strippers, but not the ones at
the places where you're charged twenty bucks to get in, twenty
bucks for some fruity fuckin' drink and they run a credit check if,
god forbid, some girl should happen to wave her ass in your gener-
al direction. No. These girls work in places with no cover, no frills
and no upward mobility. This is the last house on the block for
these girls. And every once in a while there's this exquisite beauty,
quiet, lonely, unobtrusive, you know, "Look at me if you want to,
I'll be over here." And of course you can't look away. Because she
served you coffee in the diner that morning, or she sat next to you
on the bus, or checked your groceries or came to your door offering
you a weekend with Jesus. She holds the irresistible lure of the
attainable woman. It is love. It's as real as any other . . . Who's to say
whose love is better than the next guy's. Love is love.

PROPERTY

Rosary O'Neill

Dramatic
Rooster Dubonnet, late twenties

Rooster talks about his mother and why he can't paint.

ROOSTER: Mom's a bravura figure. When you're fifteen years old and you think you can do anything, Mom is someone who can help you think you can do that. How wonderful Paris is, she'd say, and we'd be off with a maid to pack and a teacher to explain the tour. We would stand for hours before the Renoirs at the Louvre. *(Breathing deeply.)* While she studied the light and the shadow. Then we'd take a few days off and go to the Baltic Sea. The National Gallery in London. Perganon in Berlin. We'd ride in taxis above the crowd . . . stay at the Ritz. It was the white-glove approach to travel . . . breeding children who reacted to a European sensibility. *(Pause.)* I'm her last child so I ride on the cusp of her extravagance. *(Rain whistles around the house. Rubs his hands together.)* Listen to that rain. It's full of emptiness. Cold blue in the morning, bright blue at noon and intense Italianate blue in late afternoon. The walls soak up the rain. There is vermilion in the shadows, violet in the gray. Like the sound of everything that's there, that I try to paint. When you are inside the rain, there's a luminosity. I want images that have the density of rain. Nature does it easily. When you try to copy it, it's gone. Rain's not easily captured. It's the pink lie, the last little thing that crawled out of Pandora's box with all her colors. If I could paint rain the way it is, thick and smelling of oak leaves, I could jumpstart death.

PROPERTY
Rosary O'Neill

Dramatic
Bunky Dubonnet Legere, early twenties

Bunky talks about his love for the blues.

BUNKY: *(Singing.)* There's a crying Blues. A three o'clock moaning Blues. *(Hits a high note.)* That's falsetto. The deceptive voice. Nameless artists taught me that. Great unknown figures. Their families erased them after they died. If you distill Blues to a drop, it'd be a prisoner with a guitar and a hot toddy. *(Sings solo song and dances to a rap.)* Hot toddy in the cool rain. I love to sit in the rain and let the sounds come through the bones of my body like liquid music. Be there like the Mardi Gras Indians that come out to dance in the drizzle. I'd forget who I was and say, "Something is right with this picture." Sure. After the parade. How bleak it is here. Darkness and rain and funeral gloom. Day after day throughout Carnival. Never a flash of sun. I remember how I loved the parades. I'd follow them halfway to Canal Street before I realized I was tired and would have to walk back. Move in step to the hard-charging sounds. Ground moving beneath my feet. The excitement of the parades comes from the toes through the body. And the showers of trinkets from the floats. Running in the street yelling, "Throw me something, Mister." You see these floats, like beautiful swaying clouds. Soft big puffs moving down the street. You look up and feel better. Hearing the sirens, and the rush of jazz. Watching the gypsies come in and out and the Indians. Just yesterday I was a school boy. Everything was so nice. So easy . . . so . . . Football games, homecoming and sweet-sixteen parties. Convertibles and girls and . . .

RATS
Ron Fitzgerald

Dramatic
Ray, twenties to thirties

*Ray is talking to a guy who broke into his apartment about how a
little girl has brought him joy.*

RAY: It starts like this: I'm all alone on my front porch. Just sitting there.
Last sounds of summer kinda dying in the twilight. And I'm looking down the road where the sun's just about ducked behind the
hills. And I'm waiting. On something. Don't know what. But I
know it's good. Something good heading my way. And then this little girl comes along. I don't know how. Or from where. It's just —
suddenly, she's there. And she's there with me. And she takes my
hand. And I pick her up. And I bounce her on my knee. And she's
got this burning red hair. And these cool blue eyes. And she is the
most beautiful child I have ever seen. And somehow. Inside me. At
the core. I know. That she is *my* child. And that I am *her* father. And
I know . . . that she is bound for unspeakable greatness. I can see it
in her smile. I can feel it in her hands. And as we sit on our porch
looking out across that great wide world where anything is possible,
I know that she is destined to be . . . incredible. And that thought
fills me with more joy . . . than I have ever known. In my life.

THE RULES OF CHARITY
John Belluso

Dramatic
Horace, twenties to thirties

*Horace is telling his wife about what a hard day he had, pounding
the pavement looking for a job.*

HORACE: Oh. What a mess. Loretta. Are you in the bedroom? I know
you can hear me. Sound comes right through the walls in this place.
I know I shouldn't have been out so long Loretta. I went on three
job interviews, but still no job. Nothing. They all thought I was stupid. So I got a little sad. So I stole your grocery money and I went
to the bar. . . . I know you can hear me right now. I need some help.
You should've heard his voice Loretta, you should'a heard what he
said to me Loretta. That guy at the bar said, "Your voice is hurtin'
my ears, pal, keep it down!" This is what he said to me. He said I
had a loud voice, I made him take it back, I said, "A sweet lady loves
me and no sweet lady would love a man with a loud voice!" You are
that sweet lady, Loretta. And he pushed me, and I fell on my belly,
on that dusty sawdust floor, and there was that lovely song playing
on the jukebox: *(Singing the song.)*
> *"Your head is humming and it won't go*
> *In case you don't know*
> *The piper's calling you to join him*
> *Dear lady can you hear the wind blow*
> *And did you know*
> *Your stairway lies on the whispering wind."*
. . . You know that song Loretta. I know you know that song.
We made love to that song Loretta, when we first started going out,
driving around the city in my car. You remember the song. . . .
You're mad at me 'cause I got into another fight at the bar Loretta.
I cannot get up right now because of the pain in my left shoulder

Loretta. It does hurt quite a bit. I had a big fight tonight on my hands Loretta. We punched each other real hard, and then the bartender grabbed me by the shoulder and told me to calm down, he told me to listen to the jukebox, that the music would relax me; it still was playing that same song, it's a *very* long song. And I did start to calm down for a minute Loretta. I calmed down because I started to think about the time we made love to that song, the time in the backseat of my Camaro, and it was winter and you didn't want to climb into the backseat cause you knew the leather seats would be very cold but you *did* climb back there Loretta. And your eyes were wide open as we kissed soft, soft and I could see the breath floating out of your nostrils and foggin' up the back windshield. And I didn't want that to stop, no way, because that was the best, Loretta. I know you are smiling right now Loretta, if you can hear me talking about that moment then I know you are smiling, 'cause that was the best moment ever between us. I used my tongue and my breath and my finger and I made you shiver and swirl. I made you swirl, Loretta. I would have loved to just sit in that bar thinking about that moment forever, y'know? But I couldn't, 'cause I had to remember that there was an enemy of mine sitting right near me in the bar. And the song was still playing on the jukebox, but it wasn't slow and soft anymore, now it was fast and loud and *mean.* So I got up and we fought really hard, pushed and punched and he scraped a piece of broken glass across my face. That wasn't fair. That wasn't fair fighting, was it? My face is bleeding, Loretta. . . . Your darling is bleeding. I went on three job interviews, but they all thought I was stupid. *(Crying.)* My face is bleeding. Oh God. *(Horace slams his fist into the floor.)* Loretta! Come here! I'm bleeding! Loretta, you're a crazy bitch. Loretta, you're a crazy bitch.

THE RULES OF CHARITY
John Belluso

Dramatic
Paz, thirties

> *Paz, a film maker, talks about his new film, which is about what is really going on in America.*

PAZ: Well, as we all know the American Left in this country is dying, or maybe already dead. The identity politics of the late '80s and early '90s has created a fractious atmosphere which has led only towards a ghettoized discourse.

   . . . By ignoring the implications of class and economics, and focusing itself solely on the academic obsessions of cultural identity, the Left has built its own velvet-lined coffin. The assertion that the narrative of cultural identity is of paramount importance in the shaping of our new global life as citizens has created a sort of tacit endorsement of religious fundamentalism, which, along with the obvious blowback from the Reagan/Bush-era policies, led us to the Taliban and the atrocities of Ariel Sharon and, of course, 9/11 —

   . . . Think of it as a narrative about the deep, personal stories from the real people who make up the fabric of U.S. America. Sort of like Michael Moore, like that scene in *Bowling for Columbine* where he brings the crippled kids in the wheelchair to the K-Mart to return the bullets lodged in their bodies. *Fucking* brilliant. But *my* documentary, it will have my *own* unique spin. It will weave together these *stories*, these *fucking stories* that show an even *darker* side of our nation-state. A portrait of people who have been pushed and shoved by forces *way* beyond their control, and who nonetheless find a way to tap into some deep, inner, essential well of strength, and thereby rise up and transcend their social experience.

   . . . And another factor which separates this film from others of its kind is the fact that it will shift wildly in style and tone, as I am an unapologetic postmodernist. One minute funny, the next minute tragic, an emotionally eclectic roller coaster ride! And the title of my film will be *The Rules of Charity*! Because charity has rules which must be followed and if they are not followed people fall through the cracks of our so-called "social safety net" and disappear — Poof!

SCHOOL OF THE AMERICAS

José Rivera

Dramatic
Che, late twenties to early thirties

Che has been captured in Bolivia and is incarcerated in a school-house. Here he is telling the schoolteacher, Julia, about the failure of his mission and about what he knows will be his fate.

CHE: All year in Bolivia, I kept a journal of everything I thought and felt. Here's something I didn't write. Because I was too ashamed. It was a particularly bad day when we were running low on ammunition and medicine, morale was pure shit, the asthma was killing me. We hadn't recruited a single Bolivian peasant that month. My men were reduced to eating birds and monkeys and drinking their own urine. Then my horse panicked on the trail and nearly threw me. And I jumped off the poor creature and pulled out my knife — and before I knew what I was doing — I stabbed it in the chest — over and over again, Julia — there was so much fucking blood! — it was crazy! — all I wanted to do was kill everyone who betrayed us — every fucking hard-headed Bolivian in this fucking, hopeless country — then it got its blood in my eyes and mouth — I fucking swallowed it! — I was in — a rage — in a blind horrendous fucking — *(He has to struggle hard to keep control over himself — tears of rage threaten him.)* — Until my men pulled me from the screaming animal. And I suddenly felt — so sorry for it. I tried to pat his head! Can you believe that? With my bloody hands. I stroked his head, crying like a fool, until he died. And I never once cried for any man I lost. *(Beat.)* This is the kind of man you want to love? *(Beat.)* Ultimately the horse got his own revenge: from that day on, I had to walk.

. . . Ramos came in last night. Stinking drunk. Told me he'd prefer to rescue me. "Fuck Johnson! Fuck Barrientos!" But he's afraid of making a big historical mistake. Like Batista, when he set Fidel and Raul free. So he can't save me.

. . . He says the North Americans want to keep me alive to interrogate me. The final irony of my life is that I might end up in Cuba — in a prison in Guantanamo Bay! And you know what's incredible? Neither Fidel nor Brezhnev nor Mao have enough power to stop them.

SCREW MACHINE/EYE CANDY

CJ Hopkins

Seriocomic
Bob, twenties to thirties

Bob is asking some people on a game show what they'd like to talk about which might be of interest to the audience.

BOB: OK. So, let me ask you then, what *do* you want to do *here?* Tonight, I mean. Not this, obviously. What, then? Hmm? Just sit around and talk? Talk to each other? Is that what you had in mind, folks? Sit around and whine like a bunch of aristocrats? A bunch of *Russian* aristocrats maybe? No? Oh, I know. Was there some kind of *story* you wanted to tell, some *story* we haven't already heard . . . already heard a thousand times? Could it be the *story* of your troubled childhood, or of someone *else's* troubled childhood? Some tragic *story* about somebody's *son?* OK. We could try that, I guess. I'm sure the folks at home would love to see that. I'm sure they're just dying to hear every last detail of your *personal problems* in dramatic form!

. . . No? Alright. What then? Hmm. Shall we air out some sort of grievance you might have? How about it? Dan? Maura? No? Some type of *social grievance* you'd like to share? Consider your-selves representatives of some *oppressed minority,* poor *white trash,* perhaps? Like to blow off some steam?

. . . Wait, did I just say white trash? I'm sorry, actually, I mean the *middle class,* whose views I represent, of course. Oh wait, better yet, I tell you what we'll do. We'll just forget all that *heavy* stuff, and just watch ourselves a *ball game.* How about it, Dad, uh, Dan, I mean. No? Shit. OK, well, how about a nice, peaceful game of checkers then? The folks at home will just *love* watching that! That'll just entertain the shit out of folks. We'll just move the little pieces around . . . around and around in the lights all night . . . and see what pretty patterns they happen to make. It'll be, uh, *abstract,* or *conceptual,* or whatever. Or wait, hold on now, I just remembered. I think we've got a tape of the meek inheriting the earth we could run. How about it, Chip? Do we have that tape?

SONGS OF THE DRAGON FLYING TO HEAVEN

Young Jean Lee

Dramatic
White Person 2

Speaker talks about how his life is one incessant feeling of dread.

WHITE PERSON 2: I was driving over a mountain range in the middle of a golf course, and what I saw was the hole. There was a hole, and it was winking at me down there in the grass and saying, "Come here, you little piece of shit. Come out here and take a crack at me."
(He looks at White Person 1 expectantly.)

. . . I wake up in the morning with a horrible feeling, a horrible dread pushing down on me, and it's your responsibility to make me feel better about that.

(Pause.)

This is what I want from you. I want you to . . . I don't want you to have any life outside of me. I don't want you to ever go away and do something separate. I want you to be with me all the time, and for our work and pleasure to get so bound up in each other that we are never apart, having nothing uncommon and being like one person. I want to *be* you. I will never be happy until I literally become you, until I am negated, blanked-out, because everything that was once my individuality has become subsumed under yours, happily, forever. There are so many things I need to do. So many things. And I am terrified of them all, of each and every single one of them, and I feel weak, I feel unequipped to handle any of these things, so I want to run away. I want to do something that will make me disappear, that will make me feel and think nothing other than whatever it is that is making me disappear, which is you. And that is why I love you so much, because if I just cling to you hard enough in my mind, I can make myself disappear and become you.

SPAIN
Jim Knabel

Comic
Conquistador, twenties to thirties

The Conquistador has appeared in full armor in Barbara's living room. Here he tells her about the power he feels when he is armored.

CONQUISTADOR: The discovery of the New World marked a major turning point in my life. It opened up doors, gave me options I never knew I had. I found a genuine sense of purpose. I really felt like I was doing something for a change.

. . . Conquering. It is a great feeling. Meeting uncivilized people. Killing them, making them your slaves, what not.

. . . For the first time in my life, I felt good about myself. My parents were proud of me. My wife wanted to sleep with me all the time.

. . . She told me I had become so much more virile. It was true.

. . . My sexual appetite was insatiable. And I sated it quite often. Usually with my wife.

. . . Ah, the New World, the new me.

. . . This helmet.

. . . This beautiful shiny thing.

. . . Sometimes at night, I just sit on my bed and hold it on my lap.

. . . Trace the engraving. Look at my face in the reflection.

. . . Who else gets to wear something like this?

. . . The Spanish blood is strong in our veins.

. . . We go places and name them.

. . . And in the heat of battle. On my horse. This God-like thing on my head. I swing my sword down. I feel so . . . good. Really and truly good. Blessed.

. . . And afterwards. Wipe off the blood, get off my horse, stick my feet in the new earth, drink with my friends, maybe rape a prisoner.

. . . This is what I was made for. I believe that. Look at me. This is who I am. I love myself.

SPAIN
Jim Knabel

Comic
John, twenties to thirties

John has left his wife Barbara for another woman, but has come back to tell her what happened. Also in the room is a Spanish Conquistador who has appeared out of the blue.

JOHN: I met Yolanda in a snow storm. I was walking home from the Metro. She was all bundled up like an Eskimo, getting her mail I guess. Very cute. I said something stupid like: Nice snow storm, huh? She laughed. Her breath was hot. It puffed. Then she said: Do you want to come inside? And I thought she was kidding. She couldn't even see my face and I couldn't see hers. But then she took my hand and led me in. All we knew were each other's voices, but she just brought me into her house. And I started to take off my coat but she stopped me, wouldn't even let me take down the hood.

Not yet, she said, and she reached down to her pants and unbuttoned them. And I did the same with mine. And then both of us were standing with no pants or underwear in our big coats and hoods, all bundled up on top. And she pulled me against a wall and we did it like that.

The coats, you know, they were squeaking against each other. I put the hole in my hood next to the hole in hers and we breathed on each other. It was like hiding under a blanket. It was wonderful.

When it was over, she said: I will if you will. And we both took off our coats and hoods and laughed and laughed and laughed. Not because we knew each other. Because we didn't.

But then we tried to.

And I left my wife with all her books about Spain and all her misery and boredom.

But then something went wrong.

Something always goes wrong.
And here I am.
Who are you?

THE SUNSET LTD
Cormac McCarthy

Dramatic
White, fifties to sixties

> *Speaker is in the apartment of a black man who has prevented him from killing himself.*

WHITE: *(Coldly.)* I don't believe in God. Can you understand that? Look around you man. Can't you see? The clamor and the din of those in torment has to be the sound most pleasing to his ear. And I loathe these discussions. The argument of the village atheist whose single passion is to revile endlessly that which he denies the existence of in the first place. Your fellowship is a fellowship of pain and nothing more. And if that pain were actually collective instead of simply reiterative then the sheer weight of it would drag the world from the walls of the universe and send it crashing and burning through whatever night it might yet be capable of engendering until it was not even ash. And justice? Brotherhood? Eternal life? Good god, man. Show me a religion that prepares one for death. For nothingness. There's a church I might enter. Yours prepares one only for more life. For dreams and illusions and lies. If you could banish the fear of death from men's hearts they wouldn't live a day. Who would want this nightmare if not for fear of the next? The shadow of the axe hangs over every joy. Every road ends in death. Or worse. Every friendship. Every love. Torment, betrayal, loss, suffering, pain, age, indignity, and hideous lingering illness. All with a single conclusion. For you and for every one and every thing that you have chosen to care for. There's the true brotherhood. The true fellowship. And everyone is a member for life. You tell me that my brother is my salvation? Well then damn him. Damn him in every shape and form and guise. Do I see myself in him? Yes. I do. And what I see sickens me. Do you understand me? *Can* you understand me? . . . I'm sorry.

THE THIRTEENTH OF PARIS

Mat Smart

Dramatic
Jacques, thirties to forties

Jacques is offering some solace to a lovelorn man.

JACQUES: It does not matter if Annie has slept with one man or one thousand men. Everyone must find their own way with love. It is not for you to judge. And it does not give you permission to speak without dignity.

Be quiet now. Listen to how you should speak to a woman.

. . . Please forgive me for interrupting you, but I couldn't help but wonder who it is you are writing to.

. . . Please forgive me for speaking so boldly, but I think there is very little in this world that is more wonderful than a beautiful, young woman sitting alone in a café writing a letter.

. . . I thought, most likely, that you are writing a letter to your beautiful, young husband even though you will see him this evening. He will come home tonight from the office and you will embrace each other and then you will tell him you have written him a letter today, at the café, as you do everyday. He will say that you did not need to write him a letter but it makes him very happy that you have. And you will stand together on the balcony, your arms around him, and he will read this letter you have written and his eyes will fill with tears and you will hold him tighter and tighter as he reads further and discovers how your love for him has somehow grown deeper since breakfast that morning. And when he is finished, he will kiss your lips and then whisper in your ear —

. . . "My lovely wife — I must confess — I have written a letter to you as well. It is not as eloquent as yours because I am a simple man — the only eloquence in this letter is because of the love I feel for you — and please forgive the stain of yogurt on the second page. I wrote it on my lunch at the shop and spilled a drop of my yogurt on it."

. . . And your husband will carefully take the letter from his breast pocket and place it in your hands. And then you will continue to stand together on the balcony, his arms around you, and you will read this letter he wrote to you, and you will smile at the yogurt stain

and laugh at the silly jokes

and you will be delighted to discover that his love for you has somehow grown deeper since breakfast that morning

and when you are finished, you will kiss each other's lips and sit together on the balcony, drinking red wine and laughing until long after the sun has set.

So please forgive me for interrupting you, but you see, there is very little in this world that is more wonderful than a beautiful, young woman sitting alone in a café writing a letter — and very little that is more sad than an old man sitting alone in a café petting his dog named Oscar — an old man who has waited much too long and has been much, much too picky in his life and so he has never married and never found the love that he imagines is possible. It is a sad story, but he is happy enough being sad. He would certainly be more sad if he had married a woman he did not love with a love like the love he imagines is possible. So alas, the old man sits alone at a café wondering who the beautiful, young woman sitting alone at the café is writing her letter to.

THIS BEAUTIFUL CITY

Steven Cosson and Jim Lewis

Dramatic
Alt Writer, twenties to thirties

Speaker lives in Colorado Springs, which, to his dismay, has practically been taken over by evangelical Christians.

ALT WRITER: I grew up here. I left, but then my wife and I moved back with our son. We came back to be near my mom. And my stepdad, who's my dad's lover. No, my dad's dead. And my mom's a lesbian. Yeah. Yeah. *(Laughs.)* So, I came home in 2001 and around that time New Life was getting huge — Ted Haggard — and, you know, they built that monstrosity of a building out there. *(Clarifying.)* In the North. *(Pointing.)* This way. No, that's . . . Look, let me help you, it's easy. You've got the Rockies and Pikes Peak in the West, right, so that'll always be there to orient you, you'll see them wherever you are. And then in the North East in the middle of nothing, there's New Life and Focus on the Family — Focus on the Family? It's like the biggest conservative Christian media empire in the world. Yeah. Carson that's Army, Ent Air Force Base due East and inside the mountain is . . . Did you like, read anything before you came here? Ok, so also up North on the other side of the highway you've got the Air Force Academy. And the South is Fort Carson . . . there's actually four military installations. Right, Air Force Academy, Fort

But this is a beautiful place. The Mountains. It's beautiful. Did you know Katherine Lee Bates wrote the words to "America the Beautiful" here. From the top of Pikes Peak looking back on the Great Plains. Yeah, she did. This town could have been like Santa Fe. And if Focus on the Family didn't have their cross-shaped castle up there overlooking the city, I think we would have had a much bigger boom in tech in the nineties. But again, they got here first, amendment two happened, yeah which banned any kind of gay rights. Colorado Springs got boycotted. This is back in 1992. And that was it, Colorado was the Hate State and we were Jesus Springs. And now it's like I'm living in Middle Earth or something. Like everyone here's sort of . . . "Mordor is over there and we're all just outside the gates living in the shadows of Mordor." You know? I guess my point is that I think so much of the power of the Evangelicals is imaginary. It's extremely inflated. But we *give them* their power cause people are afraid. You know, like the local printers here will refuse to print something if they think it'll offend Focus on the Family. 'Cause Focus will find out and cancel their orders. And that's a lot of money. So yeah Dobson and their ilk — they're bullies. But it only works if people allow themselves to be bullied. People just roll over and bam they give up their freedom.

UNCONDITIONAL
Brett C. Leonard

Dramatic
Spike, twenties, Black

Spike is talking to his boss, who knows he skimmed some of the money off a deal they just did.

In the middle of the room Spike practices his golf swing with a 6-iron.

SPIKE: You know that nigga only quarter black, right? One quarter, ya know that shit? He half Thai, quarter black, an' quarter white, or Indian, Filipino, some'n. You see this swing, man? Shit is smooth, right? Got me that Vijay swing, look — uggh — poetry — speakin' a BLACK, that nigga Vijay? He darker than I am. Mahatma Vijay. Alright, watch this shit with the putter. Mandingo Vijay. Nigga, you watchin'? Keith — watch me drain this shit.

(Spike has put the 6-iron back in the bag and taken out a putter. He lines up over a ball. Keith is busy re-counting stack after stack of money.)

Keith? You takin' notes, bro?

. . . Uggh — dead center, baby — never up, never in — like your sex life, right Keith? Keith, you hear me? Never up, never in? I said kinda like your dick, bro — prolly whatchoo do with all that money, huh? Prolly make book so you can buy Levitra, Viagra an' shit, ol' mothafuckah. Yo! Keith! Ai'ght nigga — countchyer lil' money then, I ain' give a fuck — wha' I care — I'm a golfin' nigga — workin' on my game. Twenny-seven feet, uugh, St. Andrews.

(He misses.)

Shit, you see that? You ain't see shit, nigga — you too busy up in yo' own shit. Fitty feet, Pebble Beach.

(Lines up another.)

82

Ya know, I useta know a girl in high school named Levitra — true story — biggest whore on Campus — prolly mighta even fucked yo' ol' ass, nigga.

Where you go ta high school at, huh? Where you go? You like from Vermont or some shit, right? Huh? Yo' ass be like Colorado — Montana, maybe — some white mothafuckah state.

WELCOME HOME, JENNY SUTTER

Julie Marie Myatt

Dramatic
Buddy, twenties to thirties

Buddy is giving a sermon.

BUDDY: I, I uh — *(Buddy clears his throat for his sermon.)*

I want to thank ya'll for coming out today. I see a few new faces in the crowd, and that always makes my morning. Not because I think I'm something special or anything, or that ya'll have come to hear me say something important, because I probably won't say something all that important, I mean, unless it strikes you as such, and that would be great, but, you know, I like to keep expectations low . . . keep the expectations low, but the spirits high . . . that's kind of my philosophy . . . keep your life above any kind of expectations and you just might not be disappointed . . . (I'm already rambling.) . . . Whew . . . OK . . . The reason I like to see new faces out here is that I think, hey, look there, some folks are gonna meet some new people, maybe find a new friend, maybe find something in common, maybe share a story out here at Slab City. That's a pretty good start to a day, I think. A new friend. A common interest. A story you haven't heard before. I mean, you really can go to bed after that. Your day is complete. Good night, Irene. Or Jim. Or Mabel. Whatever your name may be. Sleep tight, with your new experience under your pillow. Maybe the tooth fairy will come leave you a quarter for it. Before it slips away . . . Which makes me think about someone.

(Buddy takes a sip of water from a bottle.)
That's good water.
(Buddy reads the label on the bottle.)
"From the majestic mineral springs of central Arkansas."

Central Arkansas. Huh. I've been there. Didn't know they had mineral springs there . . . Must be hidden . . . Where was I . . . Oh, right. I was thinking of a man named Larry Larson. Larry Larson and his wife, Susan, drove their RV out here once. Stayed about a month or two. They were from some place in . . . let's see . . . Ohio, I think . . . Now, as I quickly learned, Larry didn't care much for his oldest daughter's personality. He'd tell you that, straight out, first thing, "I have four daughters. Three of them I get. One of them is a complete mystery. A foreigner. I don't know what planet she came from, but I think it's full of hippies, communists, and nincompoops." That was how he'd speak of his oldest daughter Janet. Now I never met Janet, but I suppose if I were her, that kind of thing might hurt my feelings. But Larry Larson didn't care. He never had one thing good to say about her: "She's crazy. She's needy. She hugs too much. She talks my f-ing ear off. She's pregnant with the baby of some man who makes dog sweaters for a living. She's given up all food items that begin with A and C. She's gonna have her baby on a cedar bed surrounded by the SPCA." Etc. Well. One day, while Larry Larson was here, he and Susan got a call from their daughter's husband. There had been complications during the delivery of their grandson, and Janet didn't make it. Janet died. Well, word got around, and so we all started bringing flowers to their RV. We knew they'd be heading home the next day, but we all wanted to show our respects, as best we could. Everyone liked Larry and Susan. He played a mean game of horseshoes, and she was an excellent cook. Made many meals for the hungry folks out here. As I was laying my flowers in front of his door, Larry came outside to talk to me. I stuck out my hand to shake his, and I said, "I'm so sorry, Larry. I know this is a terrible loss. I know you loved Janet." He took my hand, and he held it for a long time, and then he finally said, "I loved her more than the others. I actually loved her the best, Buddy. I just don't — didn't know how to love her as my daughter, you see. I didn't know how to love her as someone I couldn't understand. She made me uncomfortable. She embarrassed me. I thought she make me look bad. Because she was never just a person coming into a room, she was an experience. She brought change with her. She brought laughs and chaos. She was never predictable. Something always happened when she was around. Something interesting . . . I sure hope my grandson is like her. I do. And not that damn son-in-law. He's so ordinary. I'll never know what she saw in him." Then he let go of my hand, and looked over at all the flowers in front of his RV, and I could tell he was getting ready to cry. He opened the door to go back inside. Before he closed the door he asked me to please thank everyone for the flowers and to please not let them go to waste. "Make sure those flowers get in some water, Buddy," he said. "Make sure everyone gets to enjoy them after we're gone. They paid good money for those."

(Buddy takes another sip of his water.)

I can't believe this water is from Arkansas. Unbelievable. I missed it. Huh . . . Anyway, I guess I've taken about enough of your time this morning. I've put out some coffee and it looks like someone made a delicious looking bundt cake. Thank you to whoever brought that. That took some time and generosity. And thank you to those who came out to hear me speak. I never know what I'm gonna say up here. Except welcome to the new folks. I generally wing it from there. I guess I was thinking of Larry Larson this morning because I remembered the post card he sent me last week. His grandson just turned five. And apparently, the boy talks constantly, hugs everyone he meets, and has given up all food items that begin with B and D.

(Buddy raises the water bottle in a toast:)

Amen, Larry.

WHITE PEOPLE
JT Rogers

Seriocomic
Martin, thirties to forties

Martin talks about how his daughter thinks he's really out of it.

MARTIN: Mary Esther finds my attire funny. She likes to tease me:
"Daddy's a nerd. Daddy's a stuffed shirt."

Very cute. Very endearing. She's at the age where "un-hip" and
"un-cool" are becoming part of the lexicon. But really, she's just
repeating back what she's exposed to every day. Sneering, conde-
scension — Move twelve hundred miles, you think things would be
different. People here would have more values. But it's the same
song and dance. The same rot being poured in my children's ears.

Oh, you can find it right in this office! You can feel it in the air.
Nine A.M., you walk through the halls, eyes on your back:
"Yuppie Pinhead. Sleezeball."

All the slackers. Temp employees doing us a favor just by show-
ing up and punching the clock. All these young runts with their cig-
arettes and their hipness. Trying to look like they're from L.A. or
New York. Trying to act like they're above all this, like their lives
mean something. Migrate here from some little stain of a town like
Kirksville or Ver-say-elz. Stop combing your hair, go to The Gap,
buy a black turtleneck: presto! World owes you a favor. I am not
angry, I am making a point. This fuzzy thinking, this lack of com-
mitment, it starts there and it spreads. Temps, secretaries, associates
— Not acceptable. Not on my watch. We *work* here now. None of
this coffee-donut-check's-in-the-mail — No. This is The Law.
Clarity of thought. Rigor. Language. This here: *(He gestures around
him.)* This is not like the world. This is not out there where words
have no meaning. Here there is definition: *Words are things.* Go
downstairs, walk out the door, what do you hear? Verbal diarrhea!

We open our mouths, we spew things out but we are saying nothing! Language that has no value. Words that no longer make sense. Early yesterday morning, with Mary Esther:

"Sweetie, can you pass Daddy his tan pants?"

"Those aren't tan, Daddy, those are cantaloupe." *(He gestures to his shirt.)* Look at this! You see — What? — blue shirt? No. Just ask my daughter. This is no longer blue, this is blueberry. *(His tie.)* This is not red, this is cranberry. I'm a walking fruit basket for Christ's sake! Someone is no longer Japanese, he's a Person of the Pacific Rim. It's no longer Black, it's Person of Color. What color? Fudge Ripple? Why is this? How did this happen? We are not thinking about what we are saying! We are not listening to the words we — *(He stops abruptly in mid-sentence. He looks outward. Then . . .)* This is all relevant. What I am saying has a point. If you listen . . . maybe we can find sense in this.

WILLY'S CUT AND SHINE
Michael Bradford

Dramatic
Bennet, thirties to forties

> *Bennet has a university degree but he works as a barber. Here he*
> *tells Claude a traumatic incident when he caught his wife in bed*
> *with another man.*

BENNET: *(Looking at his hands.)* Boston. That's where I was. But it wasn't about Boston. I thought once I got that piece of paper it could take me where my skin couldn't. I used to see hundreds of Mister Sylvesters on my way to the train station. And I thought, never me. I know the secret, I know the code. Have you ever seen a University degree, Claude? Sheepskin, inlaid gold leafs around the edges, letters in these huge, flourished strokes. I put it behind glass and mahogany, hung it at the foot of my bed so that I could see her reflection in it whenever she sat up on me and how unbelievably fine the light brown of her back was, mixed with that mahogany and gold, and weeks later after I went everywhere and got nowhere and doors kept shutting before I even got to them in the great North, the great land of equality, milk and honey — I was not the least bit amazed that I couldn't see her reflection because of this — pinkish looking man who was riding above her, he looked like some kind of boat on a light brown ocean. It was a long day, my skin was tired and from the doorway I could barely see flashes of her underneath him so I stepped into the room and for a moment I thought I was hoping maybe she wasn't really there. But she was. I was so surprised I stood absolutely still while he beat me nearly to death and that, Claude, is why I am here cutting heads and dispensing philosophy. What I know ain't doing nothing for me.

WITTENBERG

David Davalos

Comic
Faustus, forties to fifties

Faustus is addressing a class of college students.

FAUSTUS: "In the beginning God created the heaven and the earth." So
God existed before the beginning. So the truth of the statement "in
the beginning" is suspect. So one sentence in, our doubt is aroused.
Unless, of course, the statement is not intended to be taken literally, but rather metaphorically. But in that case, the Word of God can
be interpreted as poetry and myth. And if we can accept "in the
beginning" so easily, why not "the devil" as a name given to man's
animal nature, and "hell" as a word describing a state of mind?

Don't get me wrong: I love the Bible. It's a great read. It's got
everything: sex, violence, red dragons with seven heads. If you read
it closely enough, you can find a justification for *anything*. That's
pretty impressive — one hell of a book. But it's just that, really, only
one book, at least in the library of the philosopher. The theologian
reads it for the answers; the philosopher for the questions. They both
seek after the truth, but one stops looking when he finds this. The
philosopher, the true seeker of true Truth, continues on seeking.

I know we have some Jews and Mohammedans auditing the
class this semester — shalom, salaam — and I just wanted to make
it clear that, despite this being a Catholic university, we are not
going to be restricting ourselves to studying the philosophies of the
Church. There are, after all, more things in heaven and earth than
are dreamt of in its theology. True philosophy is like the insolent
child who, regardless of the explanation given by God the Father,
will always respond with "why?" "You must not eat from the tree of
the knowledge of good and evil, for when you eat of it you will surely die." Why? Isn't knowledge of good and evil another way of say-

ing "wisdom"? Is wisdom forbidden? Wisdom is the source of all sin? Does that sound right to you? Aristotle, on the other hand, said that "all men possess by nature a craving for knowledge," and Aristotle, of course, wasn't much of a churchgoer. He also said that one must live as either a beast, or as a god. But I say perhaps one must be both — a philosopher.

For those of you pursuing a double major — *(To Hamlet.)* and for those of you who remain undecided in your major — keep in mind that a theology degree only serves you when you're talking to God; a philosophy degree is valuable every time you talk to yourself. Of course, in my opinion, what's the difference? But then, that's my philosophy. What's yours? Choose carefully. Read, question, discuss, explore, test, doubt, defy convention. Don't settle for "because I said so," or "because that's the way it's always been." No-one has all the answers. Yet. Above all, think for yourself. Granted, about those things which we cannot think, we must believe. But about those things which we cannot believe, we must think.

WITTENBERG

David Davalos

Comic
Luther, forties to fifties

Luther is telling Faustus about his epiphany.

LUTHER: That pagan mudjuice you gave me —

. . . I love it! It's liquid manna! Not half an hour after my first sip, I felt the stirring of the Lord within me.

I'm absolutely certain of it. I was reading Paul's Letter to the Romans again for Sunday's sermon, and the same verse that always pains me became a thorn in my mind again: "For in the Gospel is the righteousness of God revealed, as it is written: 'The just shall live by faith.'" The righteousness of God — I've always read that and felt fear and anger. A righteous God, judging us all, punishing and casting us down to hell, because of our sins, sins we are damned to commit by Adam's original disobedience! I've always resented a God that would damn us to sin and then damn us for sinning. How could that be the action of a just God? I was reading it over and over, looking for a way out, any way out, and then the Lord began to move within me.

. . . I felt something awakening inside me, a quickening, something I couldn't articulate, but the stirrings of what felt like — like a revelation!

. . . At last, the moment came upon me. I ran into the privy and sat on the cold stone, but I was hot, I was sweating and my aching mind was aflame, my soul burned! I prayed for the strength to accept God's message, I prayed for wisdom, I prayed for relief! And then as I felt my bowels finally begin to empty, it was as though a bolt of divine lightning exploded in the room, my mind cleared and I felt God's grace fill me up, the cup of my soul overflowing with His sweet mercy and sublime wisdom! I saw it, I saw it writ in letters of fire, as surely as that bastard Belshazzar saw God's finger writing on his banquet wall: the "righteousness" of God doesn't mean God's inexorable justice, the way it has been taught all this time — it means God makes us right with Him, He straightens our crooked lives and justifies us to Him through our faith! As it is written: "The just shall live by faith"! Faith in His holy word, which He has given to us by His limitless grace! It's not a punishment, it's a gift! It's not about His wrath, it's about His love! I'm telling you, I wept scalding tears of joy, I felt as if I had been born again, as though the gates of Heaven had been opened and I had entered Paradise itself!

. . . The just shall live by faith! By faith alone. Faith in the holy Word of God. And then, of course, I know I must be right, because who appears at that blessed holiest moment, condensing from the stink?

. . . The old Deceiver himself, the Great Swine, the slandering Ass of Lies, rising up from his shitty pit —

. . . He wanted to catch me with my robe up, he wanted to debate, he told me my interpretation went against the church fathers, went against Aristotle! I told him Aristotle never met the Christ, and he could get acquainted with my ass!

YEMAYA'S BELLY

Quiara Alegría Hudes

Dramatic
Yelin, forties to fifties

While digging a grave Yelin tells a young man who is helping him about the day he dug his mother's grave.

JELIN: Look how I do it. You hold the shovel one hand on top, one in the middle. Put it in the dirt. Push it in with your foot. Turn the shovel and throw the dirt behind you. . . . That's right. Be precise and strong. Don't pick at it like chicken feed. You have to learn to use your strength. . . . Good. That's the way it's done. . . . When my mother died, your father and I dug the grave. Our father, your grandfather, he tried to help but he was crying the whole time. He dug with his back to us so we couldn't see. We could tell. His eyes were red and puffy. When he died, your father and me dug the grave. Just the two of us. We didn't march through town. We didn't have money to pay the priest. Then after the fire, I buried your father alone. But I thought you should be here for your mother. She would like that. . . . Sometimes you have to be like my father was. You want to cry but you turn your back and hide it. You don't let the world see. . . . When we're done, you can say something nice you remember about her. A story or something. That can be your prayer. . . . Tomorrow we'll make a cross for the graves. We'll write their names on it. Okay? . . . Answer me! . . . Answer me or I'll whack you!

RIGHTS AND PERMISSIONS

Please note:

Performance rights holder is also the source for the complete text.

THE ACTOR. © 2007 by Horton Foote. All rights reserved. Reprinted by permission of Peter Hagan, The Gersh Agency. For performance rights, contact Dramatists Play Service, 440 Park Ave. S., New York, NY 10016 (www.dramatists.com).

ADOPT A SAILOR. © 2007 by Charles Evered. Reprinted by permission of The Susan Gurman Agency. For performance rights, contact Broadway Play Publishing, 56 E. 81st St., New York, NY 10028 (www.broadwayplaypubl.com)

BOATS ON A RIVER. © 2008 by Julie Marie Myatt. Reprinted by permission of Ron Gwiazda, Abrams Artists Agency, 275 7th Ave., New York, NY 10001. For performance rights, contact Ron Gwiazda (rgwiazda@abramsartny.com).

CAGELOVE. © 2007 by Christopher Denham. Reprinted by permission of Carl Mulert, The Gersh Agency. For performance rights, contact Broadway Play Publishing, 56 E. 81st St., New York, NY 10028 (www.broadwayplaypubl.com).

THE CONSCIENTIOUS OBJECTOR. © 2008 by Michael Murphy. Reprinted by permission of Chris Till, Creative Artists Agency. For performance rights, contact Chris Till (ctill@caa.com).

DARWIN IN MALIBU. © 2007 by Crispin Whittell. Reprinted by permission of Ron Gwiazda, Abrams Artists Agency, 275 7th Ave., New York, NY 10001. For performance rights, contact Ron Gwiazda. For performance rights, contact Broadway Play Publishing, 56 E. 81st St., New York, NY 10028 (www.broadwayplaypubl.com).

DIGGING ELEVEN. © 2007 by Kia Corthron. Reprinted by permission of Bruce Ostler, Bret Adams Ltd., 448 W. 44th St., New York, NY 10036. For performance rights, contact Dramatists Play Service, 440 Park Ave. S., New York, NY 10016 (www.dramatists.com).

DOWN AND DIRTY. © 2007 by Lee Blessing. Reprinted by permission of Judy Boals, Inc. For performance rights, contact Dramatists Play Service, 440 Park Ave. S., New York, NY 10016 (www.dramatists.com).

EAGLE HILLS, EAGLE RIDGE, EAGLE LANDING. ©2007 by Brett Neveu. Reprinted by permission of Peter Franklin, William Morris Agency LLC, 1325 Ave. of the Americas, New York, NY 10019. For performance rights, contact Broadway Play Publishing, 56 E. 81st St., New York, NY 10028 (www.broadwayplaypubl.com).

ECHOES OF ANOTHER MAN. © 2007 by Mia McCullough. Reprinted by permission of The Susan Gurman Agency. For performance rights, contact Broadway Play Publishing, 56 E. 81st St., New York, NY 10028 (www.broadwayplaypubl.com).

THE EMPEROR OF ICE CREAM; or, THIRTEEN WAYS OF LOOKING AT DONALD RUMSFELD. © 2008 by Matt Moses. Reprinted by permission of the author. For performance rights, contact Broadway Play Publishing, 56 E. 81st St., New York, NY 10028 (www.broadwayplay publ.com).

FALL FORWARD. © 2008 by Daniel Reitz. Reprinted by permission of the author. For performance rights, contact Broadway Play Publishing, 56 E. 81st St., New York, NY 10028 (www.broadway playpubl.com).

FOOD FOR FISH. © 2007 by Adam Szymkowicz. Reprinted by permission of Pat McLaughlin, Beacon Artists Agency. 120 E. 56th St. #540, New York, NY 10022. For performance rights, contact Dramatists Play Service, 440 Park Ave. S., New York, NY 10016 (www.dramatists.com).

THE FOUR OF US. © 2008 by Itamar Moses. Reprinted by permission of Farrar, Straus Giroux LLC. For performance rights, contact Samuel French, Inc. (www.samuelfrench.com).

GARY. © 2007 by Melinda Lopez. Reprinted by permission of Mary Harden, Harden Curtis Assoc., 850 7th Ave. #903, New York, NY 10019. For performance rights, contact Mary Harden (mharden@hardencurtis.com).

GOOD, CLEAN FUN. © 2007 by Lee Blessing. Reprinted by permission of Judy Boals, Inc. For performance rights, contact Dramatists Play Service, 440 Park Ave. S., New York, NY 10016 (www.dramatists.com).

GREAT FALLS. © 2008 by Lee Blessing. Reprinted by permission of Judy Boals, Inc. For performance rights, contact Dramatists Play Service, 440 Park Ave. S., New York, NY 10016 (www.drama tists.com).

HUNTING AND GATHERING. ©2007 by Brooke Berman. Reprinted by permission of Seth Glewen, The Gersh Agency. For performance rights, contact Seth Glewen (sglewen@gershny.com).

THE LAST GOOD MOMENT OF LILY BAKER. © 2007 by Russell Davis. Reprinted by permission of The Susan Gurman Agency. For performance rights, contact Broadway Play Publishing, 56 E. 81st St., New York, NY 10021 (www.broadwayplaypubl.com).

MASSACRE (Sing to Your Children). © 2007 by José Rivera. Reprinted by permission of John Buzzetti, The Gersh Agency. For performance rights, contact Dramatists Play Service, 440 Park Ave. S., New York, NY 10016 (www.dramatists.com).

MAURITIUS. © 2007 by Madwoman in the Attic, Inc. Reprinted by permission of the Theresa Rebeck. For performance rights, contact Samuel French, Inc., 45 W. 25th St., New York, NY 10010 (www.samuelfrench.com).

MEN OF STEEL. © 2007 by Qui Nguyen. Reprinted by permission of the author. For performance rights, contact Broadway Play Publishing, 56 E. 81st St., New York, NY 10021 (www.broadwayplaypubl.com).

NOVEMBER. © 2008 by David Mamet. Reprinted by permission of Ron Gwiazda, Abrams Artists Agency. For performance rights, contact Samuel French, Inc. (www.samuelfrench.com).

100 SAINTS YOU SHOULD KNOW. © 2007 by Kate Fodor. Reprinted by permission of Val Day, William Morris Agency, LLC, 1325 Ave. of the Americas, New York, NY 10019. For performance rights, contact Dramatists Play Service, 440 Park Ave. S., New York, NY 10016 (www.dramatists.com).

ON THE LINE. © 2007 by Joe Roland. Reprinted by permission of Bruce Ostler, Bret Adams Ltd., 448 W. 44th St., New York, NY 10036. For performance rights, contact Dramatists Play Service, 440 Park Ave. S., New York, NY 10016 (www.dramatists.com).

PROPERTY. © 2008 by Rosary O'Neill. Reprinted by permission of Tonda Marton, Marton Agency, 1 Union Sq. W. #815, New York, NY 10003 (www.martonagency.com). For performance rights, contact Samuel French, Inc. (www.samuelfrench.com).

RATS. © 2007 by Ron Fitzgerald. Reprinted by permission of Val Day, William Morris Agency LLC, 1325 Ave. of the Americas, New York, NY 10019. For performance rights, contact Val Day (vday@wma.com).

THE RULES OF CHARITY. © 2007 by Sarah Belluso. Reprinted by permission of Patrick Herold, International Creative Management, Inc. For performance rights, contact Dramatists Play Service, 440 Park Ave. S., New York, NY 10016 (www.dramatists.com).

SCHOOL OF THE AMERICAS. © 2007 by José Rivera. Reprinted by permission of John Buzzetti, The Gersh Agency. For performance rights, contact Dramatists Play Service, 440 Park Ave. S., New York, NY 10016 (www.dramatists.com).

SCREW MACHINE/EYE CANDY. ©2007 by CJ Hopkins. Reprinted by permission of the author. For performance rights, contact Broadway Play Publishing, 56 E. 81st St., New York, NY 10021 (www.broadwayplaypubl.com).

SONGS OF THE DRAGON FLYING TO HEAVEN. © 2007 by Young Jean Lee. Reprinted by permission of Val Day, William Morris Agency LLC, 1325 Ave. of the Americas, New York, NY 10019. For performance rights, contact Val Day (vday@wma.com).

SPAIN. © 2007 by Jim Knabel. Reprinted by permission of Ron Gwiazda, Abrams Artists Agency. For performance rights, contact Broadway Play Publishing, 56 E. 81st St., New York, NY 10021 (www.broadwayplaypubl.com).

THE SUNSET LTD. © 2007 by Cormac McCarthy. Reprinted by permission of John Buzzetti, The Gersh Agency. For performance rights, contact Dramatists Play Service, 440 Park Ave. S., New York, NY 10016 (www.dramatists.com).

THE THIRTEENTH OF PARIS. © 2007 by Mat Smart. Reprinted by permission of Carl Mulert, The Gersh Agency. For performance rights, contact Broadway Play Publishing, 56 E. 81st St., New York, NY 10021 (www.broadwayplaypubl.com).

THIS BEAUTIFUL CITY. © 2008 by Steven Cosson and Jim Lewis. Reprinted by permission of Jason Cooper, Creative Artists Agency. For performance rights, contact Jason Cooper (jcooper@caa.com).

UNCONDITIONAL. © 2008 by Brett C. Leonard. Reprinted by permission of Judy Boals, Inc. For performance rights, contact Judy Boals (judy@judyboals.com). The entire text has been published also by Smith and Kraus, Inc. in *New Playwrights: The Best Plays of 2008.*

WELCOME HOME, JENNY SUTTER. © 2007 by Julie Marie Myatt. Reprinted by permission of Ron Gwiazda, Abrams Artists Agency, 275 7th Ave., New York, NY 10001. For performance rights, contact Ron Gwiazda (rgwiazda@abramsartny.com).

WHITE PEOPLE. ©2007 by JT Rogers. Reprinted by permission of John Buzzetti, The Gersh Agency. For performance rights, contact Dramatists Play Service, 440 Park Ave. S., New York, NY 10016 (www.dramatists.com).

WILLY'S CUT AND SHINE. © 2008 by Michael Bradford. Reprinted by permission of the author. For performance rights, contact the author (mbradford@hotmail.com).

WITTENBERG. © 2007 by David Davalos. Reprinted by permission of Mary Harden, Harden Curtis Assoc., 850 7th Ave. #903, New York, NY 10019. For performance rights, contact Mary Harden (mharden@hardencurtis.com).

YEMAYA'S BELLY. © 2007 Quiara Alegría Hudes. Reprinted by permission of Bruce Ostler, Bret Adams Ltd., 448 W. 44th St., New York, NY 10036. For performance rights, contact Dramatists Play Service, 440 Park Ave. S., New York, NY 10016 (www.dramatists.com).